# SpringerBriefs in Business

More information about this series at http://www.springer.com/series/8860

José Luis Retolaza · Leire San-Jose
Maite Ruíz-Roqueñi

# Social Accounting for Sustainability

## Monetizing the Social Value

Springer

José Luis Retolaza
Deusto Business School, ECRI Ethics in Finance & Social Value
Bilbao
Spain

Leire San-Jose
University of the Basque Country (UPV/EHU), ECRI Ethics in Finance & Social Value
Bilbao
Spain

Maite Ruíz-Roqueñi
University of the Basque Country (UPV/EHU), ECRI Ethics in Finance & Social Value
Bilbao
Spain

ISSN 2191-5482 ISSN 2191-5490 (electronic)
SpringerBriefs in Business
ISBN 978-3-319-13376-8 ISBN 978-3-319-13377-5 (eBook)
DOI 10.1007/978-3-319-13377-5

Library of Congress Control Number: 2015949505

Springer Cham Heidelberg New York Dordrecht London


Printed on acid-free paper

Springer International Publishing AG Switzerland is part of Springer Science+Business Media (www.springer.com)

# Acknowledgments

The authors are grateful to Lantegi Batuak, Viviendas Municipales de Bilbao, Formació i Treball, Museo de la Mineria del País Vasco, Fundación Argia and Euskaltel for their insightful comments. We would like to thank Chris Pellow for English editing and his helpful comments, as well. Moreover, this book has been possible because of the great effort and the enthusiasm of the responsible of Springer editorial. This work is part of the research group ECRI Ethics in Finance and Social Value (GIU 12/58), and it is supported by UPV/EHU research project (UFI 11/51 IEAE) and FESIDE (BOPV 20.01.2014). We also want to thank Cistercian monastery of Cardeña Community and the Darden Business School, for providing, respectively, the environment in which much of the book was written and concluded.

# Contents

# Chapter 1
# Introduction

The University of the Basque Country and the University of Deusto have been working with other social actors for more than four years via the ECRI (Ethics in Finance and Social Value) Research Group on systematically modeling the monetizing of the social value generated and distributed by different organizations. The findings obtained are methodologically robust, and have enabled an integrated accounting model to be developed in which the social value and economic value generated by organizations for their stakeholders as a whole can be considered jointly (*Blended Value*).

The conventional, monist prospective focuses solely on the value generated by firms for shareholders (Friedman vs. Freeman), so the fundamental indicators of value are financial in nature. Based on the ontological stakeholder view (Wood 1991; Mitnick 1994, 2000; Retolaza and San-Jose 2011; San-Jose and Retolaza 2012; Retolaza et al. 2014, 2015) a broader concept of value can be considered that extends in two directions, including the value distributed to all stakeholders on one side and incorporating not-directly-economic effects caused by organizations to their various stakeholders on the other. This gives rise to a more comprehensive concept of value generated, which we refer to here in general as "Social Value", though it could also be called extended value, blended value, broad value or even social income.

This book both analyses the state of the art in regard to the quantifying of social value and summarizes the various methods that are being used in practice to quantify that value (Tuan 2008; Olsen and Galimidi 2008; Wood and Leighton 2010; Mulgan 2010), going into more depth in regard to those which focus on economic evaluation.

The method proposed is based on four assumptions: stakeholder theory (Freeman 1984), the action research method (Lewin 1946), the phenomenological perspective (Husserl 1990, Tarde 1902; Polkinghorne 1989), and fuzzy logic (Zadeh 1965; Kaufmann and Gil Aluja 1986). It is developed on the basis of cost-benefit analysis (Mishan 2007), and gives rise to an overall, integrational model that we call the "Polyhedral Model" (SPOLY). This model is structured in three complementary dimensions: economic value with social impact (which we also refer to as socio-economic value), socio-economic return for the public administration, and specific social value or "social value in the strict sense". The



J.L. Retolaza et al., *Social Accounting for Sustainability*,
SpringerBriefs in Business, DOI 10.1007/978-3-319-13377-5_1

study presents motivated proposals for mechanisms capable of monetizing these values and for consolidating them in a single, overall social value, thus facilitating the processes of identifying value variables, selecting proxies, and consolidating them by means of algorithms drawn up for that purpose.

To check the applicability and practical usefulness of the method, it is tested on the ground in various organizations. We provide data and graphics taken from the foundations Lantegi Batuak and Argía, from the public sector housing management organization Viviendas Municipales de Bilbao, and from private companies Euskaltel and Formació i Treball.

Our findings reveal that it is possible for social and mercantile organizations and public administrations to autonomously quantify the social value that they generate, to integrate it as a management indicator with a view to improving their impact on society, and even to give social matters a central role in their organizations. In the conclusions to our study we reflect on the usefulness of a methodological proposal of this type, and on the possibility of scaling and standardization through a community of users.

The study comprises 8 chapters. The first is this introduction; the second examines the current situation as regards social accounting and its grounding in theory. The third describe the main problem. Chapter 4 looks in greater depth at the assumptions underlying the model proposed—action research, stakeholder theory, the phenomenological perspective, and fuzzy logic—in the context of an analytical/synthetic method. Chapter 5 reviews the methods used to date. Chapter 6 sets out the Polyhedral Model as an underlying model that can support the process of social monetization, Chap. 7 examines the variables and relationships involved, and look at its practical implementation. Chapter 8 presents our conclusions and then, they are included the bibliographical references. The study is rounded off by two annexes intended to help stakeholders identify value variables.

## References

Freeman RE (1984) Strategic management: a stakeholder approach. Pitman, Boston

Husserl E (1990) Ideas pertaining to a pure phenomenology and to a phenomenological philosophy: studies in the phenomenology of constitution. Springer

Kaufmann A, Gil Aluja J (1986) Introducción de la teoría de los subconjuntos borrosos a la gestión de las empresas. Santiago de Compostela, Spain, Milladoiro

Lewin K (1946) Action research and minority problems. J Soc Issues 2(4):34–46

Mishan Q (2007) Cost benefit analysis, 5th edn. Routledge, New York

Mitnick BM (1994) Systematics and CSP: the theory and processes of normative referencing. Bus Soc 34:5–33

Mitnick BM (2000) Commitment, revelation, and the testaments of belief: the metrics of measurement of corporate social performance. Bus Soc 39(4):419–465

Mulgan G (2010) Measuring social value. Stanford Soc Innov Rev 8(3):38–43

Olsen S, Galimidi B (2008) Catalog of approaches to impact measurement: assessing social impact in private ventures. The Rockefeller Foundation, New York

Polkinghorne DE (1989) Phenomenological research methods. In: Valle RS, Halling S (eds) Existential-phenomenological perspectives in psychology: exploring the breadth of human experience. Plenum Press, New York

Retolaza JL, San-Jose L (2011) Social economy and stakeholder theory, an integrative framework for socialization of the capitalism. CIRIEC-España, Revista de Economía Pública, Social y Cooperativa 73:193–213

Retolaza JL, San-Jose L, Ruiz-Roqueñi M (2014) Ontological stakeholder view: an innovative proposition. Glob Bus Rev 15(1):25–36

Retolaza JL, Ruiz-Roqueñi M, San-Jose L (2015) An innovation approach to stakeholder theory: application in Spanish transnational corporations. Revista Brasileira de Gestao de Negocios

San-Jose L, Retolaza JL (2012) Participation of stakeholders in corporate governance: foundation ontological and methodological proposal. Universitas Psychol 11(2):619–628

Tarde G (1902) Psichologie economique. Féliz Alcan, Paris

Tuan M (2008) Measuring and/or estimating social value creation: insights into eight integrated cost approaches. (Working Paper 12/15/08). Bill and Melinda Gates Foundation University Press. Retrieved 16 April 2014 from https://docs.gatesfoundation.org/Documents/wwl-report-measuring-estimating-social-value-creation.pdf

Wood DJ (1991) Corporate social performance revisited. Acad Manage Rev 16(4):691–718

Wood CJ, Leighton D (2010) Measuring social value the gap between policy and practice. Demos Press, London

Zadeh LA (1965) Fuzzy sets. Inf Control 8:338–353

# Chapter 2
# Background: Social Role of Companies and Success Indicators

**Abstract** The basic function of any organization, i.e. that which legitimizes it socially, is to create value for society as a whole; however concern for the economic and financial factors involved in all trading activities has resulted in the development of accounting focused on these instrumental issues. The successful development of this accounting has led to results concerned with the actual purpose of organizations being relegated or overshadowed. This chapter analyses the different theories that make economic results a good indicator or social value: transaction cost theory, contract theory, agency theory, etc. These are contrasted with a system-based outlook taken from stakeholder theory, seen as a more suitable paradigm for understanding the inherent nature of organizations and their consequent function in society. Finally, the main indicators being developed are reviewed in an attempt to visualize the social value generated fundamentally by companies.

**Keywords** Social value · Stakeholder theory · Social accounting · Monetizing social value · Value for stakeholder · Theory of the firm · CSR · Corporate social responsibility

Ever since companies as we now know them first emerged in the Industrial Revolution they have been seen as generators of economic value (Groth et al. 1996), and their social functions have been relegated to a secondary level with indeterminate effects (Fernandes et al. 2011). The economic approach adopted from the outset has led to economic results, and more specifically financial results, being overvalued, and to social outcomes being considered as a mere extension of those results consisting even in the best cases of a mere distribution of the economic value generated. Economic theorists have, more or less explicitly, taken on board the argument that the "invisible hand" (Smith 1776) socially redistributes the economic value generated. As a result better and more and more sophisticated accounting systems have gradually been drawn up that enable us to capture a "true picture" of companies. However that picture refers only to their economic functions (Gassenheimer et al. 1998). In recent years calls have been made, with some degree of success, for the role of companies as generators of not only economic but also social value to be considered (Argandoña 2011; Jensen 2001; Melé 2002, 2009; Retolaza and San-Jose 2011; Retolaza et al. 2015), and for these two values to be



J.L. Retolaza et al., *Social Accounting for Sustainability*,
SpringerBriefs in Business, DOI 10.1007/978-3-319-13377-5_2

combined into a single integrated or blended value (Prahalad 2006; Porter and Kramer 2011; Emerson et al. 2003).

Is worth pointing out that the idea of production activities having a social value is not new (Dood 1973); it can be found in publications dating from long ago (Aquinou 1954). However, it was in the wake of the Industrial Revolution that the idea gathered strength (Smith 1776), in both classical economics (Smith 1776), and Marxist thinking (Marx 1844). The earliest modern examinations[1] of the concept of social value consider it clearly from a subtractive perspective (Coase 1960), highlighting the social costs linked to negative externalities, especially in regard to the environment. Subsequently there has been a shift towards a more positive approach to the generation of social value by organizations, with the emergence of the social and non-profit sectors leading, in mercantile affairs, to concepts such as CSR (Carroll 1979; Husted and Allen 2007), corporate citizenship (Néron and Norman 2008), and stakeholder theory (Freeman 1984), where economic value is limited in the worst-case scenario and in other cases becomes merely instrumental, as in the ontological stakeholder view (OSV).

To date, the traditional view has focused exclusively on the value generated by companies for their shareholders, so the basic value indicator is profit after interest and taxation. However, based on the ontological view of stakeholder theory (San-Jose and Retolaza 2012; Retolaza and San-Jose 2011; Retolaza et al. 2015), a broader concept of value needs to be considered. The concept needs to be broadened in two directions: on one side there is a need to integrate economic value distributed to stakeholders as a whole, whether at the end of an operating period (taxes, dividends, reserves) or throughout the process of conducting economic activities (wages, social spending, taxes, R&D, etc.). On the other side there is a need to consider the not-directly-economic effects of an organization's actions on its various stakeholders. Such effects may be positive or negative (see Fig. 2.1).

Traditional theories of the firm incorporate the assumption that the only production factor that assumes residual risk is capital (Coase 1937), since other factors or resources have remuneration that is agreed on a contractual basis (Williamson 1979, 2002). Accordingly, residual profit and decision-making rights concerning management correspond exclusively to capital. However, these assumptions no longer seem to be entirely correct. On the contrary, capital can be considered as just one more production factor in regard to the generating of value, and the fact that its returns are variable does not entail any qualitative shift in regard to other stakeholders, a large part of whose remuneration may also be variable in the present or, undoubtedly, in the future since it depends largely on the results of the organization. The current economic crisis has also shown without a shadow of a doubt that residual risks are certainly not borne exclusively by shareholders but are rapidly transferred to other stakeholders: employees are fired or go unpaid, suppliers must put up with delays in payment and growing default rates, customers find themselves unable to claim on warranties, amounts owed to the public administration cannot be paid, and

[1]We consider this to mean events from the mid 20th century onwards.

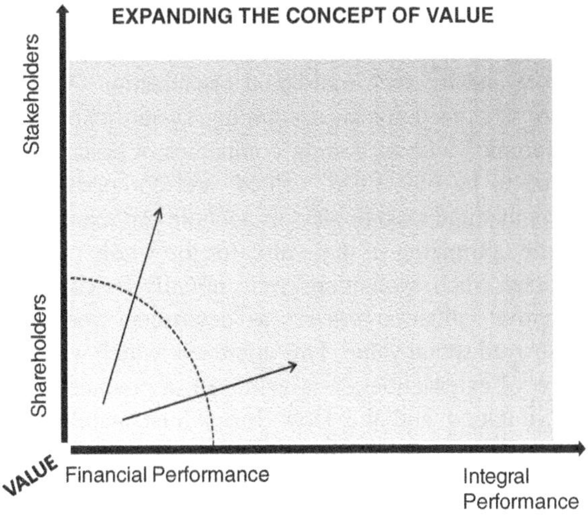


**Fig. 2.1** Concept of social value. Financial versus blended results

costly bailouts must be funded by the public as a whole. These are just some of the residual risks externalized by capital holders. If the activities of the company entail the transfer of risks to a broad group of stakeholders, then why not examine what value is generated for them, even if it is only to determine whether that value offsets the potential costs entailed by the risks run. We might even consider that each individual stakeholder is capable of valuing their own risk/benefit matrix, given that public administrations (and through them the general public) are stakeholders in all organizations, and may therefore legitimately seek to learn the balance between creation and destruction of value at each individual organization. Indeed, the contractualist view (Donaldson and Dunfee 1994) holds that social value is the only moral justification for the existence of trading companies.

To date there has been little research into the monetizing of social value, and most of the papers published have focused on quantifying impacts (Barraket and Yousefpour 2014; Murphy and Ackermann 2014). The few publications that refer to the monetizing of those impacts are mere ad hoc justifications or are still at a very early stage of development. Although the concept of social value dates back a long way in economics (Schumpeter 1909; Tool 1977), there is as yet no standard way of evaluating it. Today's CSR frameworks are an attempt to establish a set of standards and regulations to objectify the concept (Gawel 2006); however, there are presently more than 300 such frameworks (Mazurkiewicz 2004). Although expectations have grown up that GRI may be a step towards standardization in regard to accounting (Tapscott and Ticoll 2003), the truth is that so far no regulations have been established in regard to monetizing indicators, and given that GRI is being developed as a framework for presentation rather than valuation such regulations are unlikely to be created. It is true that GRI4 and integrated reporting seemed to be heading towards some degree of homogenization and standardization of indicators that will, at some point, require a modernization of units of measurement, i.e. the monetization of social value (GRI 2013).

Explicit recognition for the social function of firms leads to concern for determining the quality and quantity of the social value generated by organizations as a whole and by each individual organization (Vancaly and Esteves 2011). Just as there is a need for an accounting system capable of showing and managing the economic value of trading companies, a system is required that can enable social value to be objectified, valued, and compared so that different organizations in particular and stakeholders as a whole can manage their actions in a way conducive to the optimizing of that value for the whole of the society in which organizations operate. Such evaluations were initially based on a dichotomy, with positive and negative valuation criteria to determine whether an organization generated or destroyed social value. This approach, which was influenced to a great extent by the view of externalities, was validated in practice by well-known indices such as the FTSE4Good and the Dow Jones Sustainability Index, and by actions such as "ethical investments" and "fair trade". Subsequently, it was realized that progress needed to be made in identifying and quantifying the social value created by organizations, and the preparation of social reports or balance sheets was proposed (Bebbington et al. 2014; Fifka 2012). This required progress in terms of unifying regulations and criteria for preparation and presentation. The GRI (www.globalreporting.com) is perhaps the most highly structured example of this.

In spite of the progress entailed by the second type of feedback, there are still major shortcomings such as the following: (1) there is a great deal of room (too much) for interpretation in regard to the value generated depending on the interests of the managers of the organization itself; (2) no objective analysis of the social value generated by firms is provided, so no comparative analysis of that value is possible; and (3) the information on social value is not combined with the information on financial value, or at least does not use the same language (one is qualitative/quantitative and the other is monetary), which means that they are considered as two linked but clearly distinct subsystems.

This being so, further progress seems necessary towards standardizing a relatively homogenous, universal accounting system that can enable the social value generated by organizations—or at least a Industrial Revolution that the idea gathered strength significant part of it—to be monetarized, so that economic value and social value can be combined as two complementary areas of a broader concept of overall, integrated, expanded or blended value.

## References

Argandoña A (2011). Stakeholder theory and value creation. (Working Paper IESE No. 9), IESE Business School, Barcelona, Spain

Barraket J, Yousefpour N (2014) Evaluation and social impact measurement amongst small to medium social enterprises: process, purpose and value. Aust J Public Adm 72(4):447–458

Bebbington J, Unerman J, O'Dwyer B (2014) Sustainability accounting and accountability, Routledge

Carroll AB (1979) A three-dimensional conceptual model of corporate social performance. Acad Manag Rev 4:497–505

Coase RH (1937) The nature of the firm. Economica 4(16):386–405
Coase RH (1960) Problem of social cost, the. JL Econ 3:1
Donaldson T, Dunfee TW (1994) Toward a unified conception of business ethics: Integrative social contracts theory. Acad Manag Rev 19(2):252–284
Dood (1973) Theories of value and distribution since Adam smith
Emerson J, Bonini S, Brehm K (2003) The blended value map: tracking the intersects and opportunities of economic. Social and environmental value creation
Fernandes P, Rocha J, Rodrigues F (2011) The complete ethics chain of value: from social and ethical principles to the role of the official auditing and accounting revision entities. Int J Manage Enterp Dev 10(2):216–231
Fifka M (2012) The development and state of research on social and environmental reporting in global comparison. Journal für Betriebswirtschaft 62(1):45–84
Freeman RE (1984) Strategic management: a Stakeholder Approach. Pitman, Boston
Gassenheimer JB, Houston FS, Davis JC (1998) The role of economic value, social value, and perceptions of fairness in interorganizational relationship retention decisions. J Acad Mark Sci 26:322–337
Gawel A (2006) Corporate social responsibility: standards and objectives driving corporate initiatives (working paper). UK. Pollution probe. Retrieved 4 April 2010, from http//www.pollutionprobe.org
Global Reporting Initiative (GRI) 4 (2013) G4 Sustainability reporting guidelines. Paper retrieved 10 February 2015 from https://www.globalreporting.org/resourcelibrary/GRIG4-Part1-Reporting-Principles-and-Standard-Disclosures.pdf
Groth JC, Byers SS, Bogert JC (1996) Capital, economic returns and the creation of value. Manag Decis 24(6):21–30
Husted BW, Allen DB (2007) Corporate social strategy in multinational enterprises: antecedents and value creation. J Bus Ethics 74(4):345–361
Jensen MC (2001) value maximization, stakeholder theory, and the corporate objective function. Eur Finan Manage 7:297–317
Marx K (1844) Economic and philosophical manuscripts. Early writings, 333
Mazurkiewicz P (2004). Corporate environmental responsibility: is a common CSR framework possible. World Bank, 2
Melé D (2002) Not only stakeholder interests: the firm oriented toward the common good. In: Cortright SA, Naughton MJ (eds) Rethinking the purpose of business. interdisciplinary essays from the catholic social tradition, University of Notre Dame Press, Notre Dame, pp 190–214
Melé D (2009) The view and purpose of the firm in Freeman´s stakeholder theory. Philos Manage 8:3–13
Murphy RO, Ackermann KA (2014) Social value orientation: theoretical and measurement issues in the study of social preference. Personality Social Psychol Rev 18(1):13–41
Néron P, Norman W (2008) Citizenship, inc.: do we really want businesses to be good corporate citizens? Bus Ethics Q 18:1–26
Porter ME, Kramer MR (2011) Creating Shared value. Harvard Bus Rev 4:1–13
Prahalad CK (2006) The fortune at the bottom of the pyramid. Pearson Education India
Retolaza JL, San-Jose L (2011) Social economy and stakeholder theory, an integrative framework for socialization of the capitalism. CIRIEC-España, Revista de Economía Pública, Social y Cooperativa 73:193–213
Retolaza JL, Ruiz-Roqueñi M, San-Jose L (2015) An innovation approach to stakeholder theory: application in spanish transnational corporations, Revista Brasileira de Gestao de Negocios
San-Jose L, Retolaza JL (2012) Participation of stakeholders in corporate governance: foundation ontological and methodological proposal. Universitas Psychologica 11(2):619–628
Schumpeter J (1909) On the concept of social value. Q J Econ 23(2):213–232
Smith A (1776) The wealth of nations. Cannan E (ed) 1904 Reprint. Modern Library, New York, 1937
St Thomas Aquinou (1954) Suma Teológica, vol IV. BAC, Madrid

Tapscott D, Ticoll D (2003) The Naked Corporation: how the age of transparency will revolutionize business. Viking Canada, Toronto, ON

Tool MR (1977) A social value theory in neoinstitutional economics. J Econ Issues 11(4):823–846

Vancaly F, y Esteves M (2011) New directions in social impact assessment. Conceptual and methodological advances, Edward Elgar Publishing, Massachusetts

Williamson OE (1979) Transaction-cost economics: the governance of contractual relations. J Law Econ: 233–261

Williamson OE (2002). The theory of the firm as governance structure: from choice to contract. J Econ Perspect: 171–195

# Chapter 3
# Main Problem in Displaying the Social Value Generated by Organizations

**Abstract** The main problem is that we only look systematically at the financial value created or destroyed by firms, since conventional accounting is only concerned with reflecting value for shareholders. We do not currently have instruments that provide us with an intersubjective view of the value generated or subtracted by organizations for their stakeholders as a whole; that value is not just financial but also social, environmental and emotional at least. Any proposed solution must be based on a new discourse of business as a community of stakeholders who share resources and risks to generate value, and must therefore distribute the resulting value among themselves in a balanced fashion. To that end it is necessary to develop social accounting for stakeholders and to properly standardize it so that progress can be made towards a comprehensive, intersubjective framework or value generated and distributed.

**Keywords** Social accounting · Stakeholder theory · Social value · Stakeholder accounting · Global accounting · Integrated value · Monetizing social value

The main problem in analyzing social value is that conventional methods only show the financial value generated for shareholders, i.e. the economic and social value generated for other stakeholders is not reflected in their indicators (Olsen and Nicholls 2009). A process of standardization (Nicholls 2009) is therefore needed to objectify that value. The way in which the economic value generated by a firm is measured is shown in the principles of accounting, but there is no equivalent instrument for showing the social or environmental value of a given project or organization. However, a full description of the operations of the company should involve an account of not just the value created for shareholders but also that which is created for other stakeholders. It is therefore necessary to measure the economic, social and environmental contributions made by the firm or organization. As a way of solving this problem, at least in part, we believe that it is useful to introduce the



J.L. Retolaza et al., *Social Accounting for Sustainability*,
SpringerBriefs in Business, DOI 10.1007/978-3-319-13377-5_3

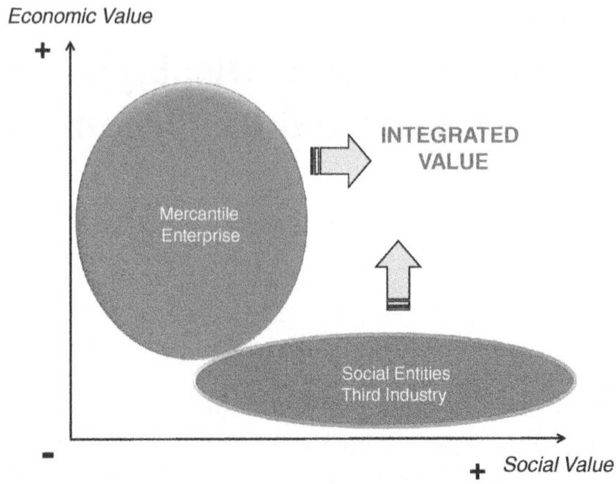


**Fig. 3.1** Blended value: economic and social

concept of "socio-economic value" (Emerson and Twersky 1996; Emerson et al. 2000), which we see not so much as income or returns for the public administration but rather as social value generated by the trading activity per se of organizations of all kinds, represented basically by wages, purchases from suppliers and investments.

Accordingly, we consider that regardless of whether their purposes are mercantile or social, organizations generate a blended value with both social and mercantile components. Mercantile operations are generally considered to be aimed at generating value for shareholders, and any value generated for other stakeholders is seen as merely residual (Friedman 1962); by contrast social or "non-profit" organizations are considered as generating social value as a priority.[1] In the approach proposed here all organizations, whatever their nature, corporate purposes or mission, are considered to generate an integrated value of which economic value and social value are constituent parts (see Fig. 3.1). That overall value must also include the emotional value generated by organizations, but the objectification and quantification of that value lies beyond the scope of this study and is therefore left open as a line for future research.

In line with the foregoing, Fig. 3.2 shows how the thesis of the separation between economic and social value needs to be replaced by a double-bottom approach or even a triple-bottom approach if the environment is factored in (Retolaza et al. 2009).

The figure above shows four possible perspectives from which social value can be viewed: the ontological view considers that the very essence of firms is linked to social value, which is what justifies the existence of firms in social and moral terms, entailing a regulatory requirement that they generate social value. It therefore seems

[1]Viewing the economic value generated by social organizations is a project in which CIRIEC has been engaged for some time via *Las cuentas de la Economía Social* ["The Accounts of the Social Economy"] (Barea and Monzón 1995).

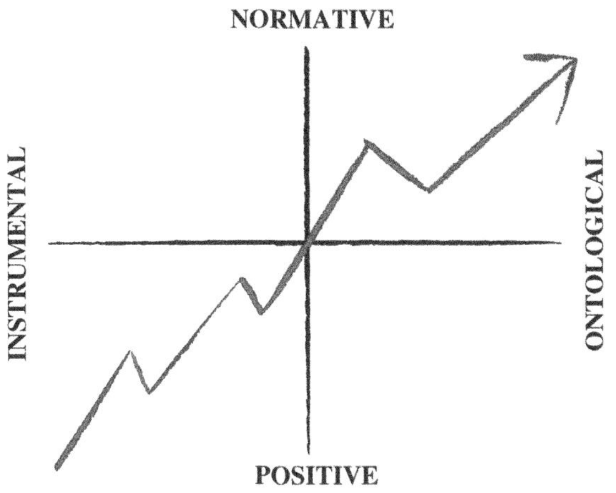


**Fig. 3.2** Four views of social value

logical for firms and other organizations to provide themselves with management tools that enable them to assess and monitor the social value that they generate, and to factor it into their management. The requirement that social value the core consideration affects not only the so-called "double bottom line" firms but requires all firms and organizations operating in the market to be capable of generating economic and social value jointly (Clark et al. 2004).

## References

Barea J, Monzón JL (1995) Las Cuentas Satélite de la Economía Social en España: una primera aproximación. Ciriec España, Valencia

Clark C, Rosenzweig W, Long D, Olsen S (2004) Double bottom line project report: assessing social impact in double bottom line ventures, Columbia Business School. Retrieved 10 April, 2014 from http://www.riseproject.org/DBL_Methods_Catalog.pdf

Emerson J, Twersky F (1996) New social entrepreneurs: the success, challenge and lessons of non-profit enterprise creation. San Francisco

Emerson J, Wachowitz J, Chun S (2000) Social return on investment: exploring aspects of value creation in the nonprofit sector. Chapter 8, pp 131–173. The robert enterprise development fund. Retrieved November 1, 2013 from http://www.redf.com

Friedman M (1962) Capitalism and freedom. University of Chicago Press, Chicago

Nicholls A (2009) 'We do good things, don't we?': 'blended value accounting' in social entrepreneurship. Acc Organ Soc 34(6):755–769

Retolaza JL, Ruiz-Roqueñi M, San-Jose YL (2009) CSR in business start-ups: An application method for stakeholder engagement. Corp Soc Responsib Environ Manag 16(6):324–336

# Chapter 4
# Methodological Proposals

**Abstract** A number of prior assumptions are needed to develop and consolidate any method for monetizing social value. Those assumptions may be implicit or explicit. We believe that explicitly expressing the assumptions that underlie the proposal for monetization is an essential step in enabling discussion to take place on elements that will be determinant in the resulting model. The model proposed here is based generically on two major research frameworks: the analytic-synthetic method, which consists of splitting a problem into its elementary component parts, analyzing them separately and then integrating them into a relational model; and cost-benefit analysis, which entails analyzing the gap between the inputs used and the outputs obtained, which enables efficiency analysis to be incorporate in the form of a ratio which, in the case of multiple factors, is developed in a Data Envelopment Analyst (DEA) framework. Four assumptions are made here: first, action research as a methodological process, with a mixed working team comprising persons who are active as actors in the organization investigated, in progressive improvement cycles normally on an annual basis. The second assumption is stakeholder theory, so each firm is considered as a network of stakeholders who contribute resources and risks for the joint generation of value which is subsequently passed on to the stakeholders as a whole. Social value, strictly speaking, is the value generated for stakeholders. The third assumption is a phenomenological outlook, under which the value variables identified are quantified in line with the value perceived by stakeholders. The fourth and final assumption is fuzzy logic, i.e. the values identified are not exact scores but centroid guidelines in a set of fuzzy data, on which upper and lower bounds of belonging are imposed.

**Keywords** Analitic-sintetic methodology · Cost-benefit analysis · Efficiency analysis · Action research · Staeholder theory · Value for stakeholders · Phenomenology perspective · Fuzzy logic



J.L. Retolaza et al., *Social Accounting for Sustainability*,
SpringerBriefs in Business, DOI 10.1007/978-3-319-13377-5_4

**Fig. 4.1** Four methodological assumptions

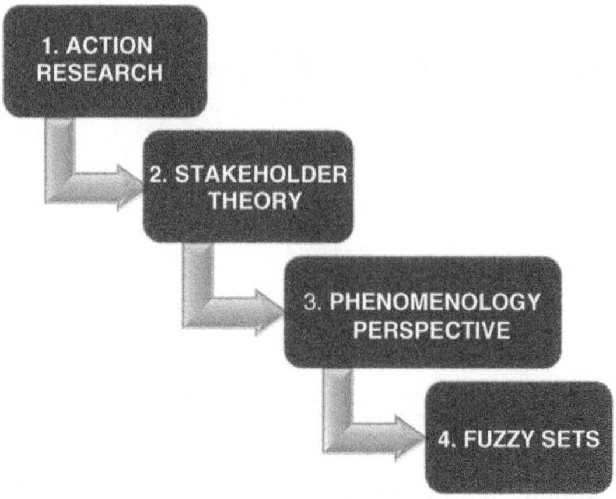


The four methodological assumptions on which the SPOLY method is based are discussed the order indicated in Fig. 4.1.

## 4.1 Action Research

Action research is defined as "a participatory, democratic process concerned with developing practical knowing in the pursuit of worthwhile human purposes, grounded in a participatory worldview which we believe is emerging at this historical moment. It seeks to bring together action and reflection, theory and practice, in participation with others, in the pursuit of practical solutions to issues of pressing concern to people, and more generally the flourishing of individual persons and their communities" (Reason and Bradbury 2007). This method was introduced by social psychologist Kurt Lewin in 1946. Lewin argued for basic research oriented towards practical application, on the grounds that it is impossible to know human beings aside from their environment and surroundings. This is in line with the ideas of Spanish philosopher and essayist Ortega y Gasset, who wrote "I am myself and my circumstances" (Ortega y Gasset 1914). In this sense action research is a form of research that links the study of problems in a given context with processes of social action oriented towards change, resulting simultaneously in increased knowledge and social change, with the actors involved leading the process of construction of knowledge and intervention in reality. In short, the idea is to reconcile theory and practice. Accordingly, a participative process of action research takes the form of eight successive steps: (1) Existence of a gap or dissatisfaction; (2) identification of a problem; (3) redefinition of that problem in terms of an active solution; (4) formulation of various hypotheses; (5) selection of one hypothesis; (6) implementation of actions to enable hypotheses to be compared; (7) assessment of the effects of action; (8) generalization by means of inductive or deductive processes.

There are three prerequisites for a process of action research (Carr and Kemmis 1986):

1. The research project must entail a social challenge with potential improvements;
2. The project must proceed progressively in a loop structure comprising planning, action, feedback and reflection;
3. The project must take place collaboratively, bringing together all the actors involved and, at least progressively, all those affected.

We believe that the main characteristics of this method can be summed up as follows: (1) Process: Action research is a work in progress. This can be linked with processes for continuous improvement of quality and with the strategic learning school (Mintzberg et al. 2005). (2) Participation: Action research must be a collaborative process [the collaborative economy (Rifkin 2014)] aimed at empowering and improving the community [Economy for the Common Good (Felber 2012)]. (3) Construction: all knowledge refers to a reality constructed by the participants [constructivist epistemological phenomenological framework].

## 4.2 Stakeholder Theory

There are three ways of tackling the problem of the monetary quantification of social value. The first, which can be called "neoclassical", is based on the core role of financial value. The social function of companies is limited to generating and distributing financial value, in line with contractual and property rights theories (Friedman 1962), to the extent that the use of financial resources by companies to carry out social actions is considered as a deviation that reduces their real impact on society (Friedman 1970). From this viewpoint the social value generated can only be quantified via the operating accounts or balance sheet of the company. In general, this is the method that has been used to date.

The second method is centered on the concept of "common good". It can be traced back to Aristotle and has a long track record in modern economics, where it has been used by authors ranging from renowned classical names such as Samuelson (1954), to current researchers such as Dembinski (2009), Daly et al. (1994), Spencer and Schmidpeter (2003), and Ostrom (1999). The basic shortcoming of this method (which on the other hand has given rise to a great many theories) lies in the fact that before it can be applied to quantification an agreement must be reached as to the meaning of the concept of "common good" (Alzola 2008; Sison and Fontrodona 2012). Different cultures, religions and periods in history have seen the common good as being represented by different, and sometimes opposing, characteristics. For example, it would be hard to find anyone nowadays who defends the principles of common good proposed by Spencer (1896), even though they were hailed enthusiastically in their day. As far as quantification is concerned, the only solution may be to consider that it should be the government of each country—at least in those countries where the government is legitimately elected—or the group of supranational organizations set up by the international community that defines the common good. However, this seriously jeopardizes diversity and personal freedom, and entails a one-dimensional reductionism of the concept of common good itself.

The third method, which we believe provides the best balance between individual freedom and social responsibility, is based on the non-instrumental (regulatory or ontological) approach of stakeholder theory. Its potential stems from the fact that it enables the interests of the supposed "common good" to be specified for a limited, accessible group of stakeholders whose true interests can be identified and systemized using suitable techniques (Retolaza et al. 2015; Ruiz-Roqueñi and Retolaza 2012). The actual common good of the persons involved can thus be defined specifically in both qualitative and quantitative terms. However, from a critical viewpoint the supposed social value may be seen as limited to the interests of those persons who are involved in a specific organization, which may even be opposed to the interests of stakeholders at other organizations. It may therefore be the case that large numbers of people (non-stakeholders) are excluded from the social value supposedly generated.[1] Without seeking to minimize these problems or the practical impact that they may certainly have, and acknowledging that they may have great potential as future lines of research, it must be noted that the first problem only arises if a single parameter for social value is sought. If a plurality of stakeholders is posited, with their corresponding values, the stakeholder model has incredible potential. As far as the exclusion of the interests of non-stakeholders is concerned, opening up the concept of "stakeholders" to mean not just those involved but also those affected, and also to cover persons in the sector hitherto considered as non-stakeholders,[2] turns this into a clearly inclusive model that is easy to align with a method based on the common good.

Moreover, this approach to corporate ethics from the perspective of stakeholder theory has a feature that clearly distinguishes it from other approaches: its individual nature. Each firm, with its group of stakeholders and their interests, is unique. It is true that firms and their stakeholders are closely linked and form what can be called "ecosystems of interests" (Ostrom 1990), in which the sets of interests are limited. However at an analytical level each firm can be considered as a different unit that is liable to have to respond to a particular, specific set of interests, which may also vary over time.

This firm-centric approach from the perspective of stakeholders as a unit of analysis calls for an individualized approach to changing circumstances defined inter-subjectively by the group of stakeholders. Accordingly, the phenomenological

---

[1]Cases in point include financial exclusion, food exclusion and lack of access to medicines. Excessive emphasis on the central role of organizations as social actors can also lead to the responsibilities of the state being given up to lobbies.

[2]An example can be found in vehicle insurance in Spain: there is a sectoral organization that acts as the policy holder if no insurer will take you as a client (stakeholder). This mechanism for the sectoral integration of non stakeholders can be useful in other types of exclusion in areas such as finances and healthcare.

paradigm seems better suited than the positivist one to objectifying social value at organizations. The Fig. 4.2, taken from Easterby-Smith (1991), shows the main differences between the positivist and phenomenological paradigms.

In regard to the basic assumptions, the phenomenological paradigms, reality is constructive socially, as in our proposal for monetizing social value [Community of Users], and both the researcher and the participants form part of the process of research [Action Research]. The goal of the research is to understand the process of generation, attribution, and distribution of value so that it can be managed optimally for the group of stakeholders. Both the eclectic approach of tackling monetization and aggregate case studies are clearly identified with the phenomenological paradigm. The process of research closely resembles those used in other research of this type (Easterby-Smith and Malina 1999). It comprises five steps: use of networks, project orientation, access to data, interpretation, publication, and dissemination. The use of networks in particular is a key step not just at the commencement but also in connection with interpretation.

From the ontological viewpoint of stakeholder theory (Freeman 1984; Freeman et al. 2010; Retolaza and San-Jose 2011), each firm is its own distinct reality, in which the full set of participants creates a specific ecosystem of generation and distribution of value (economic, social and emotional). However, the various participants and stakeholders have an incomplete view of this phenomenon, since each of them views the complete system from the viewpoint of their own interests. For an overall view of the system to be obtained, the viewpoints of all the stakeholders must be integrated, or presented as a fuzzy set comprising different objectifications of the value generated. Thus, the analysis of the value of organizations requires a synthetic analytical approach, with an initial phenomenological approach from the various viewpoints of the stakeholders [analytical phase] followed by the integration of the various viewpoints into a single, complex model [synthesis phase].

**Fig. 4.2** Positivist versus phenomenological paradigm as seen by Easterby-Smith (1991)

| The positivist paradigm | The phenomenological paradigm |
|---|---|
| **Basic beliefs:**<br>-The world is external<br>-Observer is independent<br>-Science is value-free<br>**Researcher should:**<br>-Focus on facts<br>-Look for causality<br>-Try to measure phenomena<br>-Formulate/develop hypotheses<br>**Preferred research methods include:**<br>-Using concepts<br>-Taking large samples | **Basic beliefs:**<br>-The world is socially constructed.<br>-Observer is part of it.<br>-Science is value-driven.<br>**Researcher should:**<br>-Focus on meanings<br>-Look at totality<br>-Try to understand phenomena<br>-Formulate/develop ideas<br>**Preferred research methods include:**<br>-Using multiple perspectives<br>-Taking small samples |

*Easterby-Smith, M., Thorpe R. & Lowe A. (1991),* ***Management Research: An Introduction****, London, Sage.*

## 4.3 Phenomenological View

Although precursors can be found in Fitche, Schelling, Hegel, Cousin and Stumpt (Hurtado and Toro 1997), it was Husserl who systemized this approach in the field of philosophy (Husserl 1907), where it enjoyed considerable influence in existentialism. It was subsequently extended to psychology, mainly with the *gestalt* school, and to scientific research. Phenomenology can be seen as the study of phenomena as they are experienced and perceived by individuals. In its most radical, ontological interpretation, phenomenology (Echarri 1977, 1979) refrains from making judgments of any kind concerned with any potential objective reality beyond the limits of "pure" experience. However, here we limit the idea into a process that transfers the identification of social value generated from the generating organization to the subject that perceives that value. In other words, value is not generated because someone sets out to generate it but because someone perceives it as such. When that value is transferred via the market the best indicator is price, but when it is not we must still ask about the value perceived by the supposed recipients.

Phenomenology is a reflexive, descriptive method whose statements are valid in a specific time and place. The main techniques used in the phenomenological method are (Moustakas 1994) self-reporting, direct interviews, surveys, and direct observation. Here we use mainly direct interviews, supplemented by surveys, in an attempt to reach a larger group of individuals. Triangulation is desirable with the strategic and programming documentation generated by the organization on the one hand, and with direct observation on the other, though this may occasionally be replaced by accounts given by the heads of the organization (Fig. 4.3).

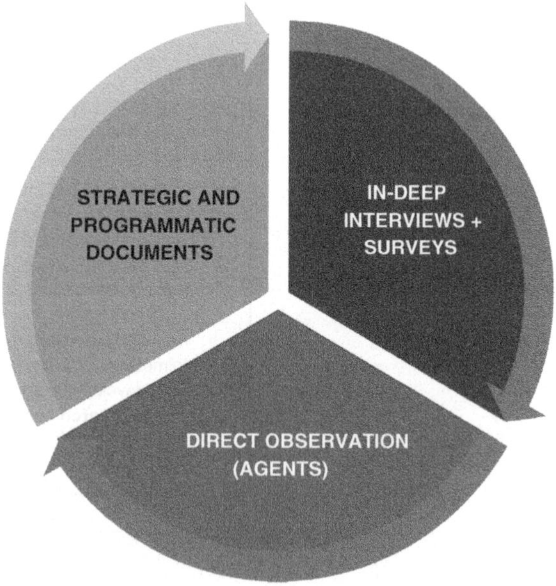


**Fig. 4.3** Triangulation process

**Table 4.1** Structure of analysis: steps

| P | Statement | Description | Application |
|---|---|---|---|
| 1 | General reading the description of each protocol | From the fact that the protocol description is as complete as possible and it does not contain spurious elements introduced clandestinely, surreptitiously or unconsciously, this time the effort will be to "immerse" in the mind map and it should be as intense as possible | Identify what respondents perceived value generated by the organization |
| 2 | Delimitation of natural thematic units | Both this step as the fifth (identification of the structure) are the two poles of the same reality. Because of this, they are closely related | Grouping of all subject areas perceived values |
| 3 | Determining the theme that dominates each unit | In this way two things are done: firstly repetitions and redundancies in each unit are eliminated, thus simplifying its extension and all the protocol | Identify the value variable that focuses each of the thematic units |
| 4 | Expression of focus on scientific language | In this step, the researcher reflects on the core issues that has reduced the thematic units (that are still written in the full language of the subject), and expressed his content in an appropriate technical language or scientific language (psychological language, educational, sociological, etc.) | Define the indicators-oriented value variables |
| 5 | Integration of all central themes in a single descriptive structure | This step is the heart of the research and of the science, because during it, it is necessary to discover the basic structure(s) of the relations of the investigated phenomenon | Value variables matrix |
| 6 | Integrate all private structures in a general structure | The purpose of this step is integrated into one description, as comprehensive as possible, the richness of the content of the structures identified in the various protocols | Integration value of the variables within the polyhedral model |
| 7 | Final interview with the subjects studied | This final step will be to perform one or more interviews with each subject to let you know the results of the investigation and hearing their views or actions against them | Returning the result and obtaining feedback which improves the process |

The phenomenological method comprises two steps: the first is the collection of information from stakeholder groups identified as recipients of value on the stakeholder map [step 1]; the second is the analytical structuring of that information [step 2]. Various points must be borne in mind when drawing up the relevant protocol: (1) show the phenomenon as it appears; (2) be as complete as possible; (3) avoid prejudices and preset categories; and (4) see the phenomenon in its natural context. In the analytical structuring step the seven steps listed in the Table 4.1 must be followed in order (Giorgi and Giorgi 2003).

## 4.4 Fuzzy Logic

One of the mainstays in the development of Western science over the centuries is undoubtedly the Law of Excluded Middle (proposition may be true or false but cannot be both at the same time). This law was apparently introduced by Chrysippus of Soli (ca. 281–208 BC) and subsequently refined by Aristotle (384–322 BC). However, as the Epicureans pointed out in their day, it is only acceptable if there is no third possibility (*Tertium Non Datur*), which is rarely if ever the case in business and economics.

Much more recently, Lukasiewicz (1878–1956) took up the thesis of the Epicureans and proposed the existence of propositions which were neither true nor false but merely "as-yet-undetermined". Based on this reasoning, he drew up the Principle of Valence ("every proposition has a truth value"), under which principles may be true (1), false (0) or as-yet-undetermined (0'5). This marked the beginning of the path towards what has become known as multivalent or fuzzy logic. Einstein pointed out that (Davies 1973) Aristotelian logic is perfectly assumable by mathematics but is harder to fit into natural science and the reality of life. In economics there are few propositions which are true or false in the strictest sense, so a shift from binary logic to multivalent logic is needed (Gil Lafuente 2001). Binary logic makes no sense in the field of the assessment of firms and the quantification of results, even if they are exclusively financial. Events and the propositions that refer to them tend to entail high levels of imprecision: the world is not black and white but made up of many shades of grey which one must know how to interpret and manage.

Imprecision means that truth is a matter of degree, at least in terms of whether an object or a variable belongs to a set. This multivalence leads to fuzzy logic, a term generally associated with any mathematical system based on fuzzy sets.

Fuzziness means multivalence, where everything is a matter of degree, including truth and falsehood in belonging to a set. In the late 20th century authors such as De Luca and Termini (1972), Kaufmann (1973), Sugeno (1977), Zimmermann (1978) and Kaufmann and Gil Aluja (1986) conducted in-depth examinations of the use of fuzzy logic in different contexts, especially in regard to business. But the benchmark author in the field is undoubtedly Zadeh, who wrote a seminal paper (Zadeh 1997) in which he pointed out that the types of object found in the real, physical world often do not have clearly defined criteria of belonging, but rather have an ambiguous status. Even so, these imprecisely defined "classes" continue to play an important role in human thinking, particularly in the fields of shape recognition, artificial intelligence, communication, information and abstraction. To deal naturally with problems in which imprecision stems from the absence of clear criteria of belonging to a class, he developed the theory of fuzzy sets, which he saw as "a step towards a rapprochement between the precision of classical mathematics and the pervasive imprecision of the real world".

By contrast with the approach taken by Wittgenstein (1988), who considered that "what can be said at all can be said clearly, and what we cannot talk about we must pass over in silence", Zadeh (1965, 1997) concludes that in complex systems precision comes into conflict with significance: the more precision, the less significance, since the significance of propositions depends not only on the indeterminacy of the variables but also on the individuals involved, and even more so on the time when they are considered. Membership of a set (a determined value) may be different at other times or if the analysis is conducted by someone else, i.e. fuzzy sets are not unique. Curiously, clear subsets are just a particular type of fuzzy subset.

Social value is clearly a system of fuzzy sets, as it is generally extremely difficult to determine whether a company creates or destroys value. Although this is a question that seems to require a yes/no answer, in fact the degree of truth depends largely on what is meant by social value, on the timing of the analysis and of the period of reference, and perhaps even on who conducts the analysis. The question of how much value an organization generates is even fuzzier: a little, some, quite a lot, a lot, a very great deal or any other category that can be thought of.

Monetizing social value seems to bring us back to a binary logic, in that it is always possible to answer yes or no in regard to whether the value generated is equivalent to a given quantity. The same seems to be true in regard to financial and economic value. However, anyone who has worked in finance will know that determining the profits for the year for the value of an asset—not to mention the value of an entire company—is an exercise in deciding between certain upper and lower bounds, which may not be clear. The timing and the people who make the decisions are key in estimating the results. As stated by Oriol Amat, at its most basic level everything is subjective. We are thus dealing with a fuzzy system.

In regard to social value the fuzziness is far greater. The range of variability in the possible upper and lower bounds attributable to an output is generally far greater than in the accounting limits set in financial reporting standards. In the valuation of an asset the variability may be 10 %, 15 %, 20 % or, in extreme cases, as much as 50 %; but the variability in the value attributed by the administration (proxy) to the creation of a new job (value variable) can range from zero to €60,000 (actual data taken from job creation subsidies in Spain in the past decade). What answer should be given if the question is whether the creation of a new job can be assigned a value of €30,000? To answer and enable calculations to take place it is necessary to resort to the principle of gradual simultaneity, which can be expressed as follows:

"A proposal can at one and the same time the true and false, on the condition that a degree is assigned to its truthfulness and a degree to its falseness".

As a result of the fuzziness of social value, in the procedure for monetizing that value it is necessary to resort several times to instruments developed to work with fuzzy sets, particularly (1) in integrating similar variables into a single value variable; (2) in identifying outputs linked to a value variable; (3) in the relationship established between outputs and possible proxies for their monetization; and (4) in quantifying the value of the proxies selected.

The biggest problem detected in the monetizing of social value is in the relationship between outputs and proxies, for which we use the concept of affinity, (Gil Aluja 1999) defined as groupings which are homogenous at given levels, structured in an orderly fashion, that link items from two sets of different types, related by the essence of the phenomena that they represent. This concept of affinity comprises three aspects: The first is the fact that the homogeneity of each grouping is linked to the level selected. Depending on the demands for each characteristic (items in one of the sets) a higher or lower threshold level is set beyond which homogeneity is deemed to exist. The second aspect is the need for the elements in each set to be linked to one another by certain rules of nature in some cases or by human will, as in the case considered here. The third is the structure that constitutes some degree of order capable of permitting subsequent decisions, in this case concerning monetary quantification. The purpose of each grouping on the one hand, and the type and strength of the links between the elements in one set and those in the other on the other hand, unequivocally determine all the possible groupings. For Gil Aluja (1999) the problem of assignation must be approached on the basis of the existence of three, normally finite, sets of physical or mental objects. The first includes the elements to be assigned, which in our case means the outputs generated for each value variables identified. The second contains the items assigned to them, which in our case means the proxies used to monetize each output; and the third contains the items on which the process of assignment is based, which in our case means essentially similarity, which is what can be called the "assignation criteria". The theory of fuzzy sets has given rise to various techniques for structuring the relationships between these three sets. Given that the problem of disqualification of valuation generally arises when the value assigned to an output is considered to be greater than the maximum value of the range of attribution, in our study we opt in general for pessimistic criteria à la Wald (Yager 1988), largely corresponding to the max–min proposed by Kaufmann and Gil Aluja (1986), in which all the so-called "soft" (non-measurable) hypotheses are calculated by taking the maxima of the minima, which is the most prudent course of action bearing in mind the hypotheses that exist. However, when the value of the proxy is highly variable and the minimum is clearly undervalued we opt for the criterion in Hurwicz (1951), taking a combination of the optimistic and pessimistic criteria (Fig. 4.4).

The diagram above shows that in the face of a dispersal of values in the possible proxies selected, we choose as our centroid score the value that optimizes the centrality of the function of belonging. Chapter 8 shows how this type of analysis is applied in a specific example.

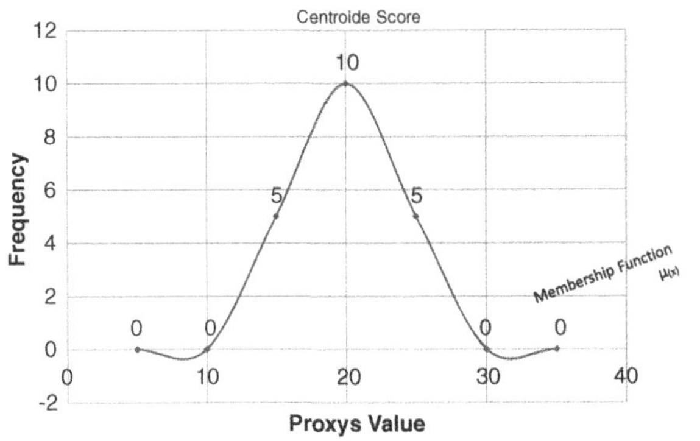


**Fig. 4.4** Optimistic criterion versus pessimistic criterion

Fuzzy logic converges particularly well with action research, because the passage of time and the succession of stages strengthen affinity links, and analysis in teams—preferably mixed teams—requires inter-subjective consensus regarding standard proxies and centroid scores.

# References

Alzola M (2008) Character and environment: the status of virtues in organizations. J Bus Ethics 78(3):343–357

Carr W, Kemmis S (1986) Becoming critical: education, knowledge and action research. Falmer Press, London

Daly HE, Cobb JB, Cobb CW (1994) For the common good: redirecting the economy toward community, the environment, and a sustainable future (No. 73). Beacon Press, Boston

Davies JT (1973) The scientific approach. Academic Press, London

De Luca A, Termini S (1972) A definition of a nonprobabilistic entropy in the setting of fuzzy sets theory. Inf Control 20(4):301–312

Dembinski PH (2009) Finance: servant or deceiver?. Observatoire de la Finance

Easterby-Smith M, Malina D (1999) Cross-cultural collaborative research: toward reflexivity. Acad Manag J 42(1):76–86

Easterby-Smith MT, Thrope R, Lowe A (1991) Management research: an introduction. Sage, London

Echarri J (1977) El mundo del físico. ed. Universidad de Deusto. Bilbao

Echarri J (1979) Humanismo científico y humanismo natural. Universidad Deusto, Bilbao

Felber C (2012) La economía del bien común. Deusto, Barcelona

Freeman RE (1984) Strategic management: a stakeholder approach. Pitman, Boston

Freeman RE, Harrison JS, Wicks AC, Parmar BL, De Colle S (2010) Stakeholder theory: the state of the art. Cambridge University Press, Cambridge

Friedman M (1962) Capitalism and freedom. University of Chicago Press, Chicago

Friedman M (1970) A theoretical framework for monetary analysis. J Polit Econ :193–238

Gil-Aluja J (1999) Elements for a theory of decision in uncertainty, vol 32. Springer Science & Business Media, Berlin

Gil-Lafuente A (2001) Nuevas estrategias para el análisis financiero de las empresas; Edición 1, Ariel Económica

Giorgi A, Giorgi yB (2003) Phenomenology en Jonathan. In: Smith A (ed) Qualitative psychology. Londres, Sage, pp 25–50
Hurtado I, Toro J (1997) Paradigmas y métodos de investigación en tiempos de cambio. Episteme, Valencia
Hurwicz L (1951) Some specification problems and applications to econometric models. Econometrica 19(3):343–344
Husserl E (1907) Die Idee der Phanomenologie. Fünf Vorlesungen, Hua II', traducción al español: Edmund Husserl, La idea de la fenomenología. Cinco lecciones, trad. Por Miguel García-Baró, F.C.E., México, Madrid, Buenos Aires 1982
Kaufmann A (1973) Introduction à la théorie des sous-ensembles flous à l'usage des ingénieurs (fuzzy sets theory)
Kaufmann A, Gil Aluja J (1986) Introducción de la teoría de los subconjuntos borrosos a la gestión de las empresas. Santiago de Compostela. Milladoiro, Spain
Mintzberg H, Ahlstrand BW, Ahlstrand B, Lampel J (2005) Strategy safari: a guided tour through the wilds of strategic mangament. Simon and Schuster, New York
Moustakas C (1994) Phenomenological research methods. Sage Publications, London
Ortega y Gasset J (1914) Ensayo de estética a manera de prólogo. Obras completas 6:1941–1946
Ostrom E (1990) Governing the commons: the evolution of institutions for collective action. Cambridge University Press, Cambridge
Ostrom E (1999) Coping with tragedies of the commons. Annu Rev Polit Sci 2(1):493–535
Reason P, Bradbury H (eds) (2007) Handbook of action research, 2nd edn. Sage, London
Retolaza JL, San-Jose L (2011) Social economy and stakeholder theory, an integrative framework for socialization of the capitalism. CIRIEC-España, Revista de Economía Pública, Social y Cooperativa 73:193–213
Retolaza JL, Ruiz-Roqueñi M, San-Jose L (2015) An innovation approach to stakeholder theory: application in Spanish transnational corporations. Revista Brasileira de Gestao de Negocios
Rifkin J (2014) The zero marginal cost society: the internet of things, the collaborative commons, and the eclipse of capitalism. Palgrave Macmillan, London
Ruiz-Roqueñi M, Retolaza JL (2012) Stakeholder marketing: a new orientation in the discipline and practice of marketing. J Mod Account Auditing 8(6):811–826
Samuelson PA (1954) The pure theory of public expenditure. Rev Econ Stat :387–389
Sison AJG, Fontrodona J (2012) The common good of the firm in the Aristotelian-Thomistic tradition. Bus Ethics Q 22(02):211–246
Spencer H (1896) Principles of ethics. D. Appleton & Company, New York
Spencer L, Schmidpeter R (2003) SMEs, social capital and the common good. J Bus Ethics 45(1–2):93–108
Sugeno M (1977) Fuzzy measures and fuzzy integrals, a survey. In: Gupta MM, Saridis GN & Gaines BR (eds) Fuzzy automata and decision processes. North-Holland, New York, pp 89–102
Wittgenstein L (1988) Investigaciones filosóficas. Crítica, Barcelona
Yager RR (1988) On ordered weighted averaging aggregation operators in multicriteria decision making. IEEE Trans Syst Man Cybern 18(1):183–190
Zadeh LA (1965) Fuzzy sets. Inf. Control 8:338–353
Zadeh LA (1997) Toward a theory of fuzzy information granulation and its centrality in human reasoning and fuzzy logic. Fuzzy Sets Syst 90(2):111–127
Zimmermann HJ (1978) Fuzzy programming and linear programming with several objective functions. Fuzzy Sets Syst 1(1):45–55

# Chapter 5
# Literature Review: Previous Methodologies

**Abstract** This chapter classifies and analyzes the main methods currently in use for quantifying the social value generated by organizations. As an aid in classification, they are grouped under five main headings: Impact Analysis, Assessment of externalities, Monetary Valuation, Management Improvements, and Rating Systems. An in-depth analysis is then conducted of the techniques of monetary valuation, and specifically of its common basis in the form of cost-benefit analysis. Two main groups are distinguished: one centered on the reduction of inputs and the other on the maximizing of outputs. In the latter a distinction is drawn between those that refer to past outputs (trading) and to future outputs (investment). Part two examines the differences between SROI as a method for analyzing return on investment and the synchronous methods of monetization of value. The essential difference is that the former operates on a set of years in which returns on investment take place and the latter focuses on the data for a past period, normally the financial year. An in-depth examination is also made of the limitations of using SROI to quantify social value generated in the past.

**Keywords** Social accounting · Cost-benefit analysis · Efficiency analysis · Monetization of social value · SROI · Social impact

In general, few social organizations systematically evaluate the social value that they generate, and the methods used vary widely even among those that do. There are three publications (Tuan 2008; Olsen and Galimidi 2008; Mulgan 2010) that summarize the main methods for analyzing social value used around the world (Table 5.1).

As can be seen, most of these methods are based on cost-benefit or cost-efficiency analysis, depending on whether outputs are considered as monetizable or non-monetizable. They can then be grouped depending on whether the operator used is a division or subtraction. In the former case the result is SROI methods, which consist of dividing the NVA (or a similar measure) by the investment required; the latter case results in differential analyses of value between the cost and the benefit obtained. This is generally referred to as "cost-benefit analysis", and entails subtracting the costs incurred from the benefits obtained.



J.L. Retolaza et al., *Social Accounting for Sustainability*,
SpringerBriefs in Business, DOI 10.1007/978-3-319-13377-5_5

**Table 5.1** Methods for analyzing social value

| Objective | Perspective | Orientation | Methodology |
|---|---|---|---|
| Impact Analysis | Quantitative (No Monetary) | | *Movement above the US $1 A Day threshold* |
| | | | *Progress out of poverty index [PPI]* |
| | | | *Dalbert approach* |
| | | | *Social value Metrics* |
| | | | *SROI calculator* |
| | | | *Common good matrix* |
| | | | *Balance social* |
| | | | *B - corp* |
| | | | *GRI* |
| | Qualitative | Preferences | *Opinion* |
| | | | *Behavior* |
| | | Satisfaction | *Life satisfaction assessment* |
| Assessment Externalities | Environment | | *Ecological footprint* |
| | | | *Trust cost PLC* |
| | | | *Environmental performance reporting system* |
| | Employment | | *Real indicators of success in employment [RISE]* |
| | | | *SROI analysis* |
| Economic Assessment (Monetary) | Reduction of inputs | Effectiveness Analysis | *Cost effectiveness analysis [CEA]* |
| | | | *Cost per impact* |
| | Incremento Inputs | | *LBG(London benchmarking group)* |
| | Increasing Outputs (Current) | Internal benefits | *Seres (McKynsei)* |
| | | | *Net benefit* |
| | | Cost benefits Analysis | *Internal return ratio [IRR]* |
| | | | *Profit / cost ratio* |
| | Increasing Outputs (Future) | Srol | *SROI framework* |
| | | | *SROI life* |
| | | | *SROI toolkit* |
| | | | *Social Impact Assessment [SIA]* |
| | Prospective Analysis | Portfolio Analysis | *Acumen fund BACO* |
| | | | *Expect return* |
| | | | *Portfolio data management system [PDMS]* |
| Management Improvement | Balanced Scorecard | | *Balanced Scorecard* |
| | Mixed | | *Charity analysis tool [CHAT]* |
| | | | *HIP scorecard and framework* |
| Rating Systems | | Dual | *B rating system* |
| | | | *Fair trade certification* |
| | | Progressive | *LEED certification* |
| | | | *Social rating* |
| | | | *Political return on investment [PROI]* |
| | | | *Development tracking system [DOTS]* |
| | | | *Foretica* |
| | | | *Corporate assessment contribution [corporate excellence]* |

SROI methods fit well into long time periods for returns (investments), while cost-benefit methods fit well in analyzing current spending. Thus, although SROI-based methods seem consistent for analyzing the relevance of investments (in parallel with the use of ROI) we do not consider them to be suitable for analyzing the value generated by ongoing projects that do not require further investment. Attempts to apply SROI-based methods to the analysis of value generation (Narrillos 2010) produce indicators whose value is doubtful and whose usefulness is scant (Javits 2008).

A suitably modified version of the impact creation chain set out in Olson and Grimaldi (2008), seems to provide a suitable framework of reference for examining the chain of social value generation, as it facilitates objectification in the identification of the inputs and outputs to be considered, which, along with monetary quantification, is one of the major problems in cost-benefit analysis concerned with social value.

The main items included in the impact creation chain are the following:

1. Inputs, in the sense of the resources needed to carry out an activity. These resources may be directly monetary but in the case of social organizations they may also be resources in kind generated on the basis of their social capital. However they need to be monetarized to enable a quantitative analysis to be carried out.
2. The activities carried out by the organization in pursuit of its goals, which can be seen as equivalent to product processing in an ordinary company.
3. Outputs for results: the results of activities carried out in pursuit of goals must necessarily be measurable, either directly or through proxies, and monetarizable.
4. Outcomes, in the sense of changes made in social systems, which may or may not be attributable to the organization under study.
5. Impacts, in the sense of outcomes attributable to the actions of the organization under study.
6. Goal alignment, in the sense of adjusting the goals of the organization to help achieve the desired impact.

As can be seen, this is a cyclical process of action, analysis and adjustment in which practical implementation and evaluation (research) are interrelated in a process of action research (Lewin 1946; Reason and Bradbury 2007).

But although the model proposed here is based to some extent on the value chain, the fact that it is a broader analysis applicable to organizations as a whole rather than just to projects means that there are also substantial differences: it blends the concept of value chain with that of social accounting. First of all, we are interested only in quantifying those inputs whose use entails a direct opportunity cost and that could be used alternatively to generate alternative social value. The possibility of there being other inputs of this type is left open, but in general we refer only to public sector subsidies. Other inputs with opportunity costs must be taken into account for analyses of efficiency in regard to social value, but are unlikely to be taken into consideration in accounting for the social value generated. Secondly, activities appear as a black box, in that it is their results that are analyzed, even though it will certainly be necessary to go back to the activities themselves when the time comes to shift from valuation to management. Thirdly, the outcomes considered as impacts (perceived value) by stakeholders are analyzed before the outputs, because only those outputs that are translated into outcomes are relevant to us. Finally, there is no sense in analyzing impacts, so our analysis focuses exclusively on the actions of organizations.

This being so, the four main methodological problems are the following: (1) identifying outcomes, which we have redefined as "value variables", and which we identify based on a phenomenological analysis of stakeholder perceptions; (2) the relationship between these value variables and the outputs generated by an organization; (3) monetizing those outputs via the use of proxies; and (4) selecting equivalent proxies or a standard reference proxy.

As is known, one of the main limitations in attempting to monetize social value lies in attributing an economic value to social assets which are hard to quantify: for instance, what is the value of a human life? However, we believe that if value is to be viewed and managed optimally a way must be found of attributing monetary value to social outputs, even if it is by means of a fuzzy proxy incapable of objectifying of value that may in itself be unmeasurable (Emerson et al. 2000). The value thus attributed is not the intrinsic value of the social asset or even its value in use: it is merely an approximate reference to the exchange value that can be attributed to it in a specific society at the time when the valuation takes place. Accordingly, a monetary approach as a reflection (albeit incomplete) of social value has certain major advantages (Scholten et al. 2006): first of all it facilitates the blending of social and economic results and their potential alignment; secondly, it contributes to transparency by identifying and clarifying outputs related to social value; and thirdly, it facilitates comparative analysis by simplifying the valuations of stakeholders and their decision-making processes.

In the conventional cost-benefit method and in the impact creation chain (Olson and Grimaldi 2008), before the impacts attributed to an organization can be analyzed the impacts not attributable to it and any collateral negative impacts generated must be subtracted from the total outcomes. That means analyzing four additional points:

1. The displacement caused (Emerson and Twersky 1996), e.g. when one person finding a job entails the exclusion of another.
2. Deadweight, in the sense of what would have happened anyway if the organization had not intervened. This entails identifying the base case scenario at the end of the process and not at the beginning (Olsen and Nicholls 2005; Nicholls 2009).
3. Attribution in the sense of the full set of inputs into the organization by third parties (which must be discounted from the outputs).
4. Drop off, in the sense of the deterioration over time of the outputs valued.

Logically, in a complex social problem interpretations and calculations concerned with displacement and deadweight are subjective, and generally controversial. This is why they are the main problem (followed by the attribution of value to social outputs) in establishing a consensus concerning the quantification of the value generated (Scholten et al. 2006). A glance at the studies published by SROI (see the papers and working documents at http://www.socialimpactscotland.org.uk/case-studies) shows that in all cases displacements are multiples of five. This can only be achieved by rough calculation.

Monetization in our model is carried out from the perspective of the organization, so as far as deadweight is concerned there is no point in considering what would have happened if the organization did not exist, because the result would always be zero value generated. Should such a case arise it would in any event affect not just social but also financial accounting.

Any displacement perceived by stakeholders would be seen as a negative variable (loss of value in the working environment). It would therefore be incorporated using exactly the same procedure as for positive variables, but with the opposite sign. In the markedly social projects with which we have worked to date there have been no negative variables (and no displacement of any kind), but such circumstances may well arise as the range of organizations for which this monetization process takes place broadens, and it could hypothetically have a significant influence at some trading companies.

In general, few social organizations systematically evaluate the social value that they generate, but among those that do a distinction must be drawn between social organizations and trading companies. The former use a wide range of methods, but among the latter—which include almost all large, listed companies—the standards used are much more consistent. There are three publications (Tuan 2008; Olsen and Galimidi 2008; Mulgan 2010) that summarize the main methods for analyzing social value used around the world. For trading companies the list of methods must be extended to include mainly the GRI, Integrated Reporting and RSC.

As shown in the graph at the beginning of this chapter, there are five main approaches to the quantification of social value, though not all are equally well developed. They are: (1) Impact analysis; (2) Evaluation of externalities; (3) Economic evaluation; (4) Management improvements; and (5) Rating systems. Impact analysis and rating systems are perhaps the most highly developed of the approaches at present, though neither of them quantifies impact monetarily. Evaluation of externalities is highly developed in the field of environmental issues, where the "ecological footprint" is used to monetize the negative impact of $CO_2$ emissions, so its use for monetizing social economic impact looks like a natural development for the near future. Proposed management improvements, for their part, refer to a natural aspiration, i.e. managing social impact. However they are relatively poorly developed in terms of methodologies, and should therefore be used after socio-economic impact analysis. Until a standardized system for monetizing social value is developed it will be difficult to manage within the strategic core of organizations. Lastly, we come to the analysis of methods for the economic evaluation of social returns, which we refer to as Monetization of Social Value. The first impression is that all these methods have resources and proven track records in terms of analysis, but that their systematic use is an aspiration rather than a reality.

Special mention must be made of two methods which are being used more and more, even though their grounding is highly questionable: the method of the London Benchmarking Group (LBG), based on the cost of resources used in specifically social ways, and the RSC method developed by McKinsey, which assesses the economic impact of social responsibility on organizations instead of assessing the impact that organizations have on society. Both these methods clearly fall within the bounds of monetization, but their approaches are very different from those which are generally accepted as ways of monetizing social value, in the first case because spending is a very remote indicator of results (because the result of management is considered as zero) and in the second case because what is analyzed is merely the benefit for the organization itself rather than benefit in relation to the social impacts generated.

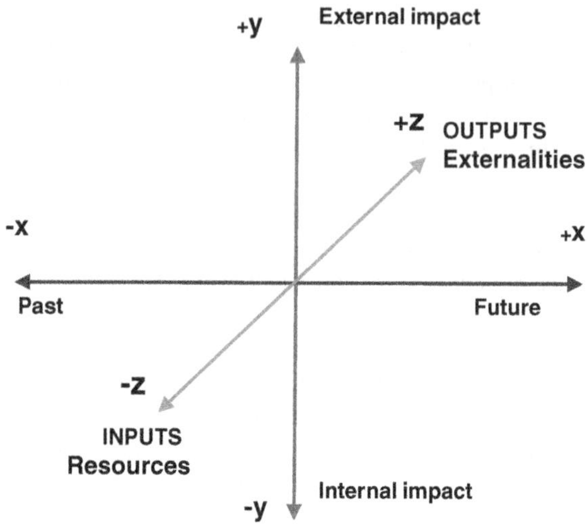


**Fig. 5.1** Input-Output versus resources-externalities: past and future

Portfolio methods focus, as classical SROI does, on the future returns of a project or organization, by contrast with accounting methods, which focus on analyzing returns in the past, normally using the financial year as a unit of measurement.

Three dimensions can therefore be considered to exist which enable all the different methods used to monetize social value at organizations to be classified: (1) past/future; (2) inputs /outputs; (3) internalized value/projected value (Fig. 5.1).

In recent times it has become fashionable, particularly in Spain, to propose SROI as the measure of the return on social value. It must be said that there is a long tradition of research into social return on public sector investment in the English-speaking world (Maass 1966), and cost-benefit analysis is a very widely used method. The graph below shows the number of papers published on this issue in high-impact journals since the 1960s (Figs. 5.2 and 5.3).

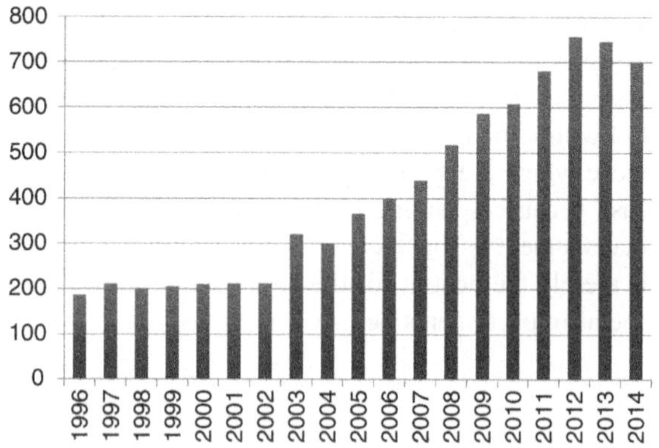


**Fig. 5.2** ISI-WoS publications (revised February 2015) with "cost-benefit" in their topics

**Fig. 5.3** ISI-WoS publications with "social return of investment" in their topics

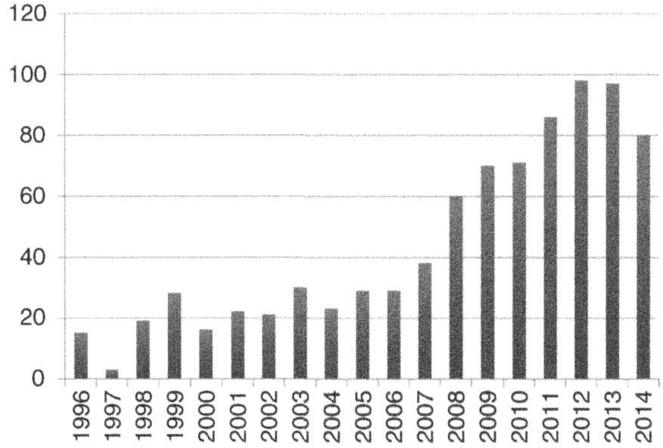


By contrast, we can find only three papers in which SROI appears as part of the title or the topic, the earliest of which dates from 2004 (Lingane and Olsen 2004). This leads us to think that there may be papers on social return on investment that do not use this particular term; however the SROI network (http://www.thesroinetwork.org/what-is-sroi/a-history-of-sroi) seems to date the origin of the term SROI to 1997, which would suggest that we are not dealing with the same concept. Indeed, SROI is presented as parallel to ROI, with financial returns (R) being replaced by social returns (SR). Based on this parallelism it seems that SROI, like ROI, serves to assess future returns on present investments. This is consistent with the introduction of terms such as displacement (Emerson and Twersky 1996), deadweight, base case scenario (Olsen and Nicholls 2005; Nicholls 2009), attribution and drop-off (Scholten et al. 2006). To the extent that we are attempting to assess future social returns on current investments, it is necessary to predict the flows of social value that can be expected over the term of the investment (as would be done with a payback period), and to find the updated value on the date on which the investment is made. Thus, to calculate the net flow of social value it is necessary to take into account (subtract) all the effects indicated above. If the problem for a part of it is displaced (Emerson and Twersky 1996), e.g. if one person finding a job means another losing his/hers, the result that would have been obtained without the intervention must be discounted (Olsen and Nicholls 2005; Nicholls 2009). To that end, highly effective methods have been developed to identify the base case scenario using synthetic control groups (Abadie et al. 2010). The need to distinguish attribution is not so clear, because what is analyzed is precisely the social return attributed to the investment in question. The same goes for drop-off: any potential drop-off during the term of the investment must already have been taken into account in the calculation of the flows.

However, this concept of SROI as parallel to ROI is only applicable if there is present investment with future results: it makes no sense if both conditions are not present. If there is no investment then any future social return would entail an infinite SROI, which is meaningless. And if the past is to be analyzed then logic requires the use of a measure of social returns parallel to those currently used in business: NVA (SNVA), IRR (SIRR). On the other hand, if the idea is really to analyze the social return on organizations and not on investment it would be hard to apply SROI, unless we started to draw inferences on the relationship between assets or current capital and possible past investments. But for that purpose other measures already exist and work well at companies when it comes to analyzing trading accounts, e.g. ROA (SROA), ROE (SROE), ROS (return on sales) (SROS), EBIT (SEBIT) and EBITDA (SEBITDA). Attempting to consider current spending as investment not only contravenes the principles of accounting and financial analysis but also complicates the analysis enormously. According to Occam's razor, i.e. the criteria of simplicity, it therefore seems much simpler to use generally accepted accounting principles adapted to social value rather than attempting to wrestle SROI into shape: attempting to use it for everything will leave it unfit for anything at all.

In Spain there is a tendency to use SROI to analyze not just investments, for which it is entirely suitable, but also the current operations of organizations (Narrillos 2010), which leads to indicators of doubtful worth and little usefulness (Javits 2008). One of the most common errors of this type of approach is to see subsidies as investments. This may be correct in the case of subsidies specifically for investment, but is entirely incorrect and indeed illegal in the case of subsidies for operations, the category into which most subsidies received by service sector organizations fall. Undoubtedly, a ratio can be obtained whose numerator is the social value generated and whose denominator is the subsidy received, but that ratio bears no relationship to the ROI in either its numerator or its denominator, and by extension no relationship to the supposed SROI. It therefore only serves to create confusion. Moreover, from a practical viewpoint it must be taken into account that any trading company that does not receive subsidies will have an infinite SROI, and any company that does receive subsidies may well have an SROI that is far higher than that obtained for social organizations. This imbalance disappears when a subtraction is used instead of the ratio.

In most projects already up and running it makes no sense to analyze social or economic investment, because interest here is not in deciding whether to invest or not but rather in quantifying the net social value generated by an organization in a given period of time. This may serve as a basis for decisions concerned with subsidies or additional funding for operations that are unlikely to be classed as investments. Cost-benefit type methods therefore seem to be more suitable for this type of analysis (Mill 2006), such as those mostly proposed by Tuan (2008). The idea is that social or socio-economic value is (like financial value at a company) obtained fundamentally from the difference between the inputs and outputs generated over a given period of time, generally one year, and that the best way of reflecting this may well be to use dynamic information systems [Social MIS] that include the relevant data (Emerson et al. 2000).

# References

Abadie A, Diamond A, Hainmueller J (2010) Synthetic control methods for comparative case studies: estimating the effect of California's tobacco control program. J Am Stat Assoc 105 (490)

Emerson J, Twersky F (1996) New social entrepreneurs: the success, challenge and lessons of non-profit enterprise creation. San Francisco

Emerson J, Wachowitz J, Chun S (2000) Social return on investment: exploring aspects of value creation in the nonprofit sector. Chapter 8, 131–173. The Robert Enterprise Development Fund. Retrieved 1 Nov 2013 from http://www.redf.com

Javits C (2008) 'Redf's current aproach to SROI'. REDF, Working Paper, available in http://www.redf.org/learn-from-redf/publications/119 (Available at 8 de December 2014)

Lewin K (1946) Action research and minority problems. J Soc Issues 2(4):34–46

Lingane A, Olsen S (2004) Guidelines for social return on investment. Calif Manag Rev 46 (3):116–135

Maass A (1966) Benefit-cost analysis: its relevance to public investment decisions. Q J Econ 208–226

Mill GA (2006) The financial performance of a socially responsible investment over time and a possible link with corporate social responsibility. J Bus Ethics 63(2):131–148

Mulgan G (2010) Measuring social value. Stanford Soc Innov Rev 8(3):38–43

Narrillos H (2010) El SROI (social return on investment): un método para medir el impacto social de las inversiones. Análisis Financiero 113:34–43

Nicholls A (2009) We do good things, don't we?: 'blended value accounting' in social entrepreneurship. Acc Organ Soc 34(6):755–769

Olsen S, Galimidi B (2008) Catalog of approaches to impact measurement: assessing social impact in private ventures. The Rockefeller Foundation, New York

Olsen S, Nicholls J (2005) A framework for approaches to SROI. DRAFT for haas social metrics conference reviewers (Working Paper). City Berkeley Retrieved 10 May 2013 from http://www.haas.berkeley.edu/responsiblebusiness/conference/documents/SROIFrameworkv.Haas.pdfSaraOlsen.pdf

Reason P, Bradbury H (ed) (2007) Handbook of action research (2nd ed.). Sage, London

Scholten P, Nicholls J, Olsen S, Galimidi B (2006) SROI a guide to social return on investment. Lenthe, Amsterdam

Tuan M (2008) Measuring and/or estimating social value creation: insights into eight integrated cost approaches. (Working Paper 12/15/08). Bill and Melinda Gates Foundation University Press. Retrieved 16 April, 2014 from https://docs.gatesfoundation.org/Documents/wwl-report-measuring-estimating-social-value-creation.pdf

# Chapter 6
# Polyhedral Model: Social Value Model for Stakeholders

**Abstract** Based on the previous analysis of the different methods for quantifying social value and the fours prior assumptions established above—Action Research, Stakeholder Theory, the phenomenological perspective and fuzzy logic—a comprehensive, holistic model is developed that we call the "Polyhedral Model". This model makes it possible to identify and then quantify the distribution of value between the various stakeholders of an organization. The consolidation of the value generated for the full set of stakeholders reflects the overall value generated by the organization. This model differs from the conventional conflict-of-interest-based approach normally associated with income distribution in that it introduces a holistic concept of value that includes at least financial value, so-called social value and emotional value, though we have been unable to draw up a model for quantifying this last type. Stakeholders do not oppose one another or necessarily converge fully in terms of perceived value; rather there is some degree of value shared between some or all stakeholders, and some degree of specific value for individual stakeholders. The more closely aligned the interests of stakeholders are, the greater the shared value and therefore the joint appropriation of value become. The less closely aligned they are, the more conflict there will be for the specific appropriation of value.

**Keywords** Social accounting · Polyhedral model · Consolidated value · Value for stakeholders · Shared value · Alignment · The social impact of economic activity · Social specific value · Socio-economic return

For social value to be measured and monetized the term "social value" first needs to be defined. Although a more detailed explanation can be found above, we feel it necessary to give a brief introductory outline here to help readers understand the model proposed. Three main approaches can be taken to calculating how much value is generated: first there is the new liberal paradigm, which holds that the best valuation is that which is made via the market, since the market actually monetizes value generated through the willingness to pay of the user. From this viewpoint there is no need to conduct any social valuation beyond the actual accounts of the business concerned, at least in regard to trading companies, though some kind of



J.L. Retolaza et al., *Social Accounting for Sustainability*,
SpringerBriefs in Business, DOI 10.1007/978-3-319-13377-5_6

valuation might be needed for organizations which are not governed by the market. At the opposite end of the spectrum is the paradigm of the "common good" (Argandoña 1998; Felber 2012; Sison and Fontrodona 2012). This system may be suitable in theory, but in practice it gets bogged down by the difficulty of defining "common good" in a way acceptable to society as a whole. Resorting to hypernorms (Donaldson and Dunfee 1994) is too theoretical, and in any event they must be drawn up by specific micronorms which are much harder to set out. References to international agreements (global compact, millennium goals, etc.) are too vague to provide a benchmark for a system of monetary quantification, and would be useful in any case only as a criterion for internal decision-making.

The third approach is stakeholder theory, and it is on this that our model is based. We believe that social value needs to be monetized as specifically as economic value is in terms of the specific value generated for shareholders of companies, but oriented towards stakeholders as a whole as the recipients of the value generated by organizations. This enables the value perceived by various stakeholder groups and the individuals of which they are comprised to be identified. Admittedly, in theory at least, the full set of stakeholders of an organization could reach an agreement concerning selfish interests that benefits them in detriment to society as a whole. However, given that stakeholders are part of society and, as a whole, represent widely differing interests; it is not easy to envisage the interests of the full set of stakeholders as being opposed to those of society. Along these lines various publications (Retolaza et al. 2015) have shown that stakeholder interests largely coincide with, or at least are not opposed to, the interests of society. Moreover, it is always possible to resort to hypernorms (Donaldson and Dunfee 1994) and to overall agreements as a criterion for goodness in regard to perceived value variables. Finally, it must be pointed out that there are also undoubtedly "non stakeholders", i.e. excluded parties (they could called "nobodies") people who are of no interest to the set of organizations in a sector, as occurs in the fields of finance or vehicle insurance, so that what we have is not so much a negative social value as the lack of a potential value. In such cases it is up to various initiatives by the public sector (regulation of the right of access to insurance for vehicles), civil organizations (ethical banking) and businesses (corporate citizenship) to make progress alone or in cooperation towards turning these "non-stakeholders" into stakeholders, and thus making them party to the social value generated.

As a result of the foregoing, the biggest problem facing a system for monetizing social value is whether certain outputs can be classed as social value or not. As pointed out above, the various outputs of an organization may be allocated social value or not depending on who the evaluator is and where their interests lie. The question of whether the production of armaments generates any social value is likely to elicit different replies from different people depending on their anthropological and social viewpoints. Replies may also vary substantially depending on whether the question is asked in peacetime or wartime, and depending on whether the scope of analysis is domestic or global. Finding a single answer linked to the common good looks like an extremely difficult task, so we have opted to approach the issue from the viewpoint of stakeholders, in line with the proposal in Argandoña

(1998, 2011). The interests of stakeholders may sometimes be selfish and dysfunctional, or even exclusive, so that the least powerful among them are relegated to the category of non-stakeholders (Melé 2002, 2009; San-Jose and Retolaza 2012), but these difficulties can be overcome by setting up levels higher than business units that enable such relegated interests (sector, state, global community) to be brought together, or that delegate the job of representing them to shapeholders (Kennedy 2013) such as the state, NGOs, international organizations, etc.

In spite of these limitations, we believe that the stakeholder view gives rise to a paradigm that has great potential for identifying social value. Such value is not universally defined in advance but refers rather to the valuation drawn up by stakeholders, or more specifically by those persons who hold an interest in a company or organization, in regard to its outputs in a given period (Retolaza and San-Jose 2011). This view is consistent with the publications by Freeman (1984) and Freeman et al. (2010) and with agency theory, to the extent that agency relationships can be considered as not being restricted solely to shareholders but extending at least to all those who have a stake in an organization and contribute to the generation of value by that organization (Jensen and Meckling 1976; Harris and Raviv 1978; Eisenhardt 1989), i.e. to the full set of stakeholders. Once the stakeholder paradox as per Goodpaster (1991) and the ungovernance problem as per Jensen (2001) have been overcome this leads to a multi-stakeholder agency theory with agents holding a trust responsibility to the full set of stakeholders. Additionally, on the basis of stewardship theory (Davis et al. 1997), in which the agent is seen as being at the service of the other stakeholders, that responsibility could be extended not just to those agents that generate value but to all those affected negatively by an organization. The method proposed here enables them to be incorporated subtractive in terms of the generation of negative value.

However the main characteristic of this view is how hard it is to generate a single value, because depending on the point of view (stakeholder group) from which the valuation is made certain outputs may or may not be considered as having social value for a particular group. This means that the same project, company or organization may be considered as having different social values depending on which stakeholder conducts the analysis. From a classical viewpoint, in which a single, objective value is considered to exist, it is no simple matter to determine a value in this case. Using fuzzy logic (Zadeh 1965; Kaufman and Gil-Aluja 1986), which we believe fits better with reality, it is possible to identify the overall social value created for the various stakeholders without assuming there to be an actual sum total of values in any case. We call the model that results from this approach the Polyhedral Model or SPOLY. It integrates stakeholder theory into an analytical-synthetic framework, from a phenomenological perspective and using fuzzy logic. Figure 6.1 is intended as an aid to understanding the model.

The different areas represent the value generated (SV) for each stakeholder (Stakeholder n°). These values are not necessarily the same: they usually match in some cases but not in others. The core represents the overall value attributed to the matching variables, which can be called the "shared value". This value is calculated by adding up all the matching values for the full set of stakeholders. In addition

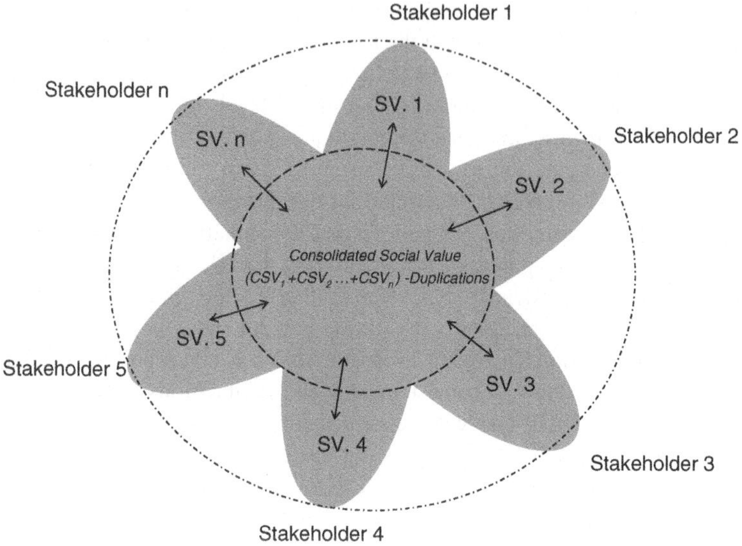


**Fig. 6.1** SPOLY polyhedral model

there are values generated for specific stakeholders that do not match those of other stakeholders. The consolidation of the total value generated by the organization for the full set of stakeholders constitutes the blended value generated. The graph is a simplification, so it does not show those values that might potentially be shared only partly by some but not all stakeholders. In the calculation system these values are taken into account and quantified.

In addition the model reveals the extent to which the interests of different stakeholders are aligned, based not on design but on results. If there is confluence between the shared value and the consolidated value then there is a greater alignment of interests among the stakeholders of the organization in question (Kaplan and Norton 2006), which means that the return perceived by each stakeholder is greater than when those values are very different from one another. It can be assumed that alignment of interests and increases in returns will help to align the resources (Peteraf 1993) linked to each stakeholder.

The SPOLY Polyhedral Model can be seen as an underlying analysis model from which a process emerges that can be applied specifically to an organization. The graph below summarizes the research micro-process that is conducted to bring about the monetization of the social value generated by an organization (Fig. 6.2).

In line with this model, the first step towards monetarizing social value is to identify the recipients of that value. This is done by organizations themselves by drawing up stakeholder maps (Fig. 6.3).

The stakeholder-centric Polyhedral Model solves the problem usually found in socio-economic impact analyses, which tend only to consider tangible costs and ignore other types of impact related to the various stakeholders or special interest

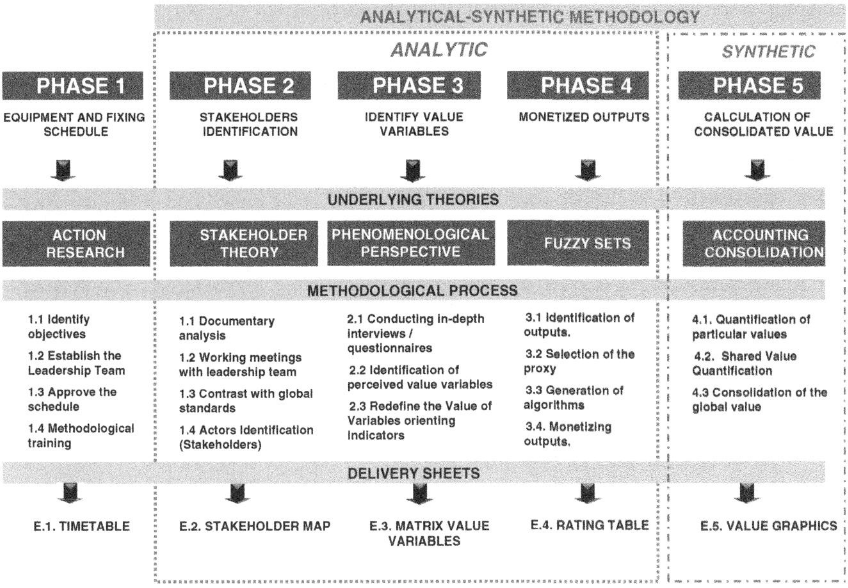


**Fig. 6.2** SPOLY development process

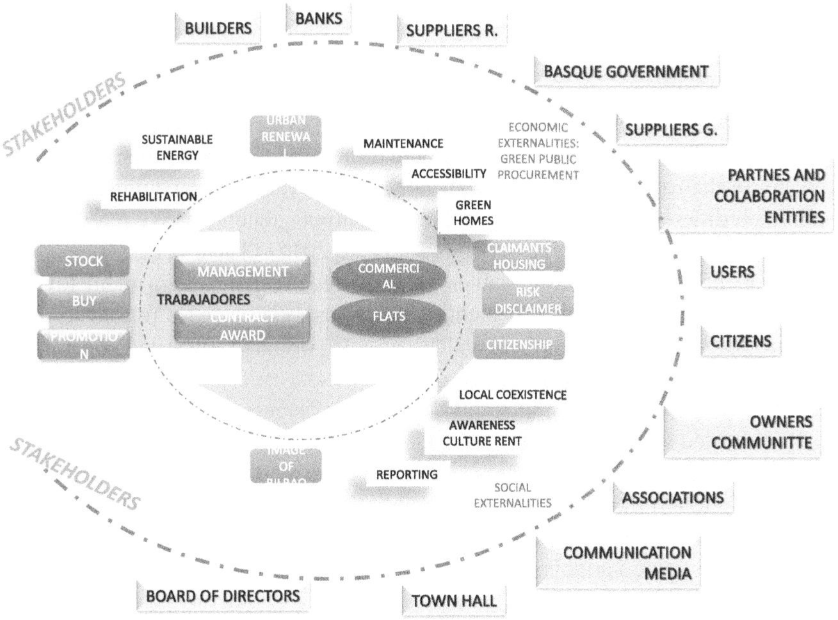


**Fig. 6.3** Example of a stylized stakeholder map

**Table 6.1** Short list of interests of the full set of stakeholders

| N° | THE JOINT INTERESTS OF STAKEHOLDERS | Civil Society | Adminis-tration | Financiers | Clients | Enterprise Groups | Trade Unions |
|---|---|---|---|---|---|---|---|
| 1 | Creating jobs for people with disabilities | | | | | | |
| 2 | Proactive anticipation of regulatory development | | | | | | |
| 3 | Positive externalities | | | | | | |
| 4 | Social peace | | | | | | |
| 5 | Transparency | | | | | | |
| 6 | Socio-economic benefits (tax saving) | | | | | | |
| 7 | Increase family income | | | | | | |
| 8 | Tractor effect on sector entities | | | | | | |
| 9 | Service + social value (client) = reinvestment in their collective | | | | | | |
| 10 | Example transformer (other companies possible) | | | | | | |
| 11 | Generate value added suppliers and customers | | | | | | |
| 12 | Increased autonomy: reduction of dependence on caregivers | | | | | | |
| 13 | Emotional value: self-esteem, tranquility, social satisfaction | | | | | | |

groups (Emerson et al. 2000). However, if the model is to be applied on the basis of the usual approach in stakeholder theory (Freeman 1984; Freeman et al. 2008, 2010) a one-to-one relationship must be assumed to exist between stakeholders and interests. In practice this is not usually the case: within the same stakeholder group diverse, and even opposing, interests may coexist. Moreover, different stakeholders may share the same interests (Ruiz-Roqueñi and Retolaza 2012; Retolaza et al. 2015). Indeed, as we were able to confirm via the in-depth interviews conducted, the same stakeholder may have different, and even divergent, interests depending on point of view. This means that in practice the model needs to be redefined in terms not of the role of stakeholders but rather of the various viewpoints of interest from which different stakeholders evaluate the outputs generated. We refer to these viewpoints as "interest variables" (Retolaza et al. 2015) (Table 6.1).

Subsequently, these value variables must be redefined to orient them towards indicators so that it is possible to identify the outputs and proxies related to them.

Figure 6.4 shows an example of value variables oriented towards indicators for the case of Lantegi Batuak.

The analyses conducted inductively show the existence of three ecosystems of social or blended value that largely coincide with those established in the theoretical part above, i.e. (1) the social value generated via economic activities; (2) the socio-economic return generated for the public administration; and (3) the specific social value generated for specific stakeholder groups. The diagram in Fig. 6.4 shows how the value variables are grouped in these three ecosystems.

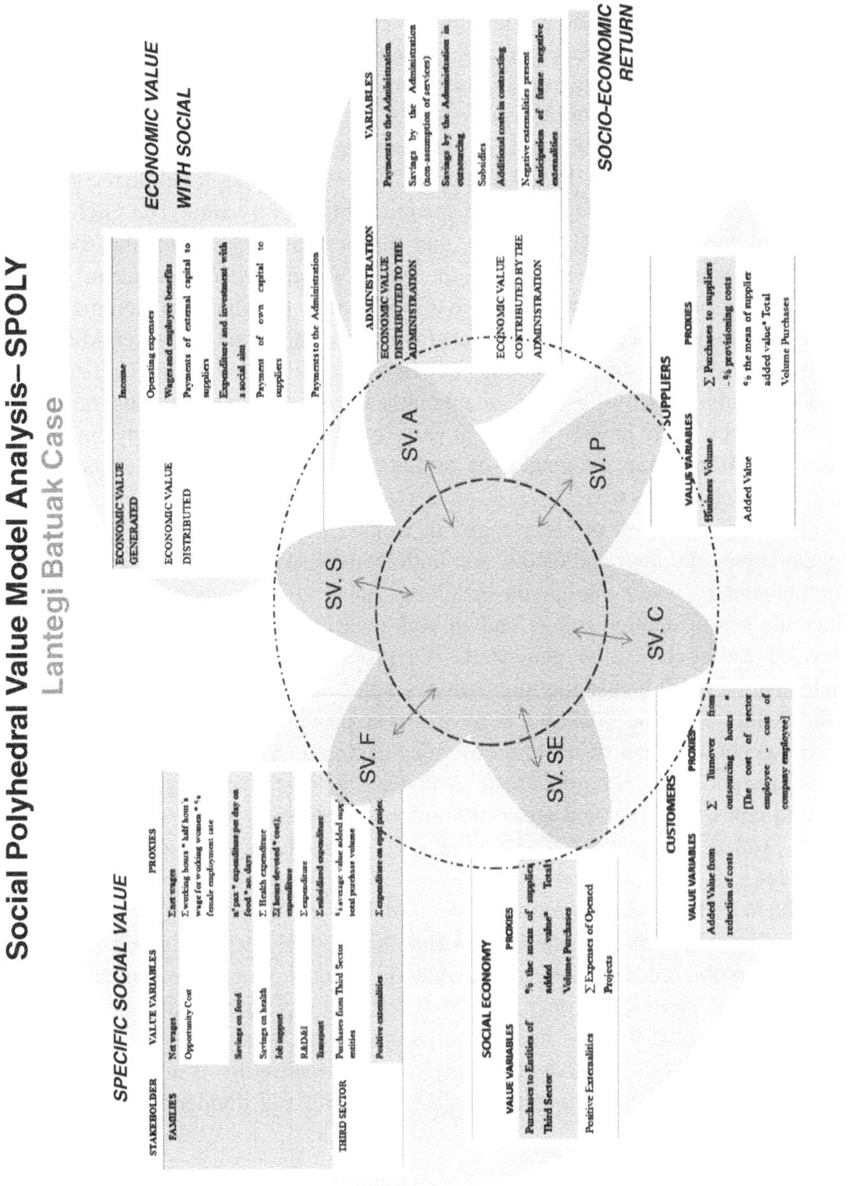


**Fig. 6.4** SPOLY model at Lantegi Batuak

## 6.1 Economic Value with Social Impact

In regard to the first system, i.e. the generation of economic value with social impact, it must be taken into account that the very raison d'être of businesses is said to be the value that they generate for society as a whole (Smith 1776). It is assumed that this is what enables them to obtain a profit on the difference between costs and revenues. Moreover, although it may not be their fundamental function they also generate social value indirectly via various outputs such as wage payments, the collection of VAT and tax levied on profits. However, although public records exist little effort has been made to date to quantify this social value. The GRI (Global Reporting Initiative) (GRI, 4) holds that the best way of calculating the social impact of economic activity is via the Cash Value Added Statement,[1] on the grounds that it is the best reflection of the extent to which an organization is committed to its respective stakeholders (Moneva et al. 2006). However AECA (the Spanish Association of Accounting and Business Administration) (Gallizo 2007) considers value added as a more suitable indicator for two main reasons: on the one hand it reflects more closely the actual value contributed by a company, and on the other it facilitates the integration of results according to geographic, national or sectoral criteria (Fig. 6.5).

From the viewpoint of fuzzy logic, in which there is no need for there to be a single value, the two indicators are both considered as suitable and mutually complementary, even though the resulting values differ considerably. However, since the transformation rule is known both measures can be used to give a better view of the social value generated. We propose that the Cash Value Added Statement (CVAS) be used in micro-analyses to calculate the value of an economic unit. In line with the GRI, we believe that it provides a better reflection of the overall generation and distribution of value captured but not necessarily added by an organization. As a complement to this we believe that macro-integration by sectors, types, geographical areas or some other criterion would work better with Value Added, since the CVAS could give a falsely broad view of the value generated.

Table 6.2 shows our proposal for the variables involved in the process. It must be taken into account that the Cash Value Added Statement is turned into Value Added by replacing income by value added in the economic value generated and at the same time subtracting operating costs from the economic value distributed. It must also be noted that we include variations in the price of the stock exchange value in payments to providers of equity capital, because this is actually at least as important as a form of remuneration as the distribution of dividends or increases in book value.

---

[1]VEGD (Economic Value Generated and Distributed). This is a statement drawn up based on a cash criterion which is relatively similar to the Cash Value-Added Statement.

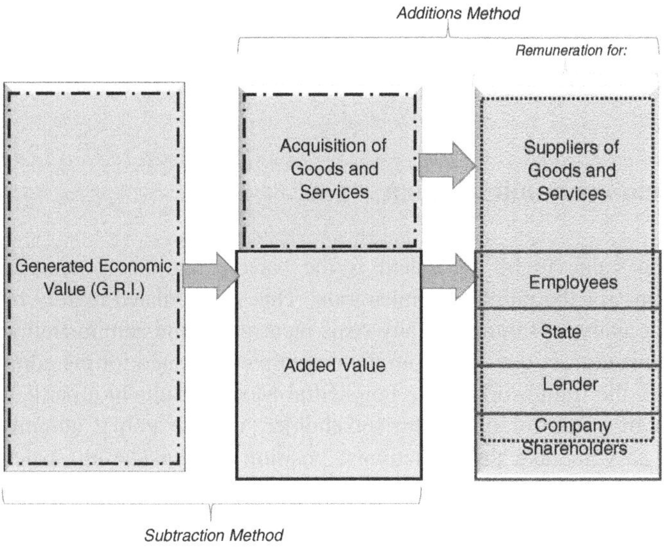


**Fig. 6.5** Economic value added versus value generated

**Table 6.2** Calculation of economic value with social impact

| | Variables | Description |
|---|---|---|
| Generated economic value | Income | Sales + net income from financial investments and sales of assets |
| Distributed economic value | Operating expenses | Payments to suppliers + non-strategic investments + easy payment |
| | Salaries and employee benefits | Total cash flows oriented workers |
| | Payments to providers of outside capital | Payments to providers of financial services |
| | Expenses and investments with corporate purpose | Voluntary contributions and investments in social improvement |
| | Payment to money funds providers | Dividends + increase reserve funds |
| | Payment to administration | VAT + Corporate tax + Other taxes |
| | Payment to own equity providers | Changes in the price of the stock value |

Adapted from GRI (2013), AECA (2002)

By adopting this model we are able to make standard calculations concerning the economic value captured by an organization and its subsequent distribution to the various social actors (socialization).

## 6.2 Socio-economic Return

The second value to be calculated is the socio-economic return generated by organizations for the public administration. This is calculated mainly by applying cost-benefit analysis, subtracting any costs incurred by the administration in regard to the organization in question from the outcomes generated for the administration. In this case, the framework of the Polyhedral Model results in a particular case of generation of value for a specific stakeholder, i.e. the public administration. It would be easy to take the reductionist position of considering society and the administration as the same thing, given that the latter is elected by the former and supposedly manages its interests. However, given that the ability of the administration to respond to all the needs and interests of society is limited, the return produced will always be less than the social value generated for the full set of social stakeholders. Table 6.3 shows the variables taken into account in this calculation.

**Table 6.3** Calculation of socio-economic return

| | Variables | Description |
|---|---|---|
| Economic value distributed to the administration | Payments to administration | VAT + Corporate tax + Other taxes |
| | Saving administration (assuming no service) | Reduction of expenses that would be forced to incur the administration if the entity does not exist/ceased to exist |
| | Management savings in outsourcing | Differential input/output relationship with the entity contracted in connection with the second highest bid |
| Economic value provided by management | Subsidies | Administration pays contributions to the institution for various items |
| | Additional costs in hiring | Increased cost for a service/product contracted in relation to the best |
| | These negative externalities | Expenses that the administration is obliged to incur for the actions of the organization in the current year |
| | Anticipation of negative externalities future | Advance prorated future costs tendered by the current actions of the organization |

## 6.3 Specific Social Value

"Specific social value" can be understood to mean the non-economic value distributed by an organization to its stakeholders. The fundamental characteristic of this value is that it can only be appreciated as such by one specific stakeholder group, and is of little or no value to others. Furthermore it is non-monetary in nature, which makes it necessary to resort to subjective proxies in order to monetize it. Table 6.4 sums up the process of identification, quantification and monetization of this type of value [SV.3], specifying at each stage the question we are attempting to answer, the method used and the results expected.

The Model comprises a succession of 10 steps:

(1) Involvement of the organization: step one comprises a shift from mere interest in the matter on the part of members of an organization to taking on board monetization of social value as an organization-wide challenge, determining the members of the working team at the highest level and setting a calendar of actions.

**Table 6.4** Process of monetization of social value: SPOLY PROCESS

| Phase | Question | Methodology | Result |
|---|---|---|---|
| 1. Implication of the organization | Who are the players involved? | Action research | Working group and schedule |
| 2. Identification of different stakeholders | Who are the recipients of the value generated by the organization? | Mind map | Stakeholder map |
| 3. Value variables identify (VV) | What it is the value given to each of stakeholder? | Interviews | List of value variables |
| 4. Value-oriented indicators of variables redefinition | How you can quantify the value derived by variables? | Expert group | Value variables matrix |
| 5. Identification of outputs generated by the organization | What output does the organization generate? | Analysis of internal information | Output list |
| 6. Identification of all social inputs used | What social inputs used the organization? | Analysis of internal information | List of social inputs |
| 7. Identification of proxies that eventually monetize inputs and outputs | How do you evaluate the outputs? | Big data | List of proxys |
| 8. Generate the calculation algorithms | How do we calculate the value of the variables? | Logic maths | Algorithms calculation |
| 9. Monetary calculation of generated social value | What is the monetization of generated social value? | Modelo Poliedrico | Poliedrical map |
| 10. Qualitative identification of non-quantifiable impacts | What aspects have not been quantified? | | Qualitative outputs list |

(2) Identification of stakeholder groups: a stakeholder map is used to identify all those groups for whom the organization could generate value and then determine what representatives of those groups will be asked to provide information.
(3) Identification of value variables (VV), mainly by means of open interviews with representatives of various stakeholders.
(4) Redefinition of value variables oriented towards indicators, which means turning the value variables obtained in colloquial terms into properly structured propositions for which comparative indicators can be drawn up.
(5) Identification of the outputs of the organization, defined on the basis of the potential indicators for a variable. These must always comprise data from the organization itself.
(6) Identification of the full set of social inputs used to calculate the net value generated. Inputs are quantified in terms of social and opportunity costs, mainly referring to public funding.
(7) Identification of proxies that enable outputs and, if possible, inputs to be monetized using a process similar to that used in corporate accounting to calculate reasonable value. Any active market data will be obtained first and if, as tends to occur with social value items, no such data exists then the valuations drawn up by the public administration or those used in similar areas under inter-subjectively agreements will be resorted to.
(8) Generation of algorithms for calculation that relate outputs with proxies in order to quantify the monetary value of each output.
(9) Calculation in monetary terms of the social value generated, consolidating the overall value of the outputs identified.
(10) Identification of non-quantifiable qualitative impacts. Not all outcomes can be quantified in monetary terms (at least we have not yet been able to do so). This category includes emotional value in particular. In the case of these non-monetizable values a qualitative list of all the outputs generated is drawn up.

### *6.3.1 Variables Involved*

In the case of specific social value there are no variables that can be identified for all types of organization: they depend on stakeholder interests and on the value variables that stakeholders perceive (Table 6.5).

**Table 6.5** Calculation of specific social value

| Specific social calculation | | | |
|---|---|---|---|
| Stakeholder | Value variables | PROXYS | Relational algorithms |

**Table 6.6** Specific social value matrix for Lantegi Batuak

| Stakeholder | Value variables | PROXIES |
|---|---|---|
| Families | Net wages | Σ net wages |
| | Opportunity cost | Σ working hours * half hour's wage for working women * % female employment rate |
| | Savings on food | No. pax * expenditure per day on food * no. days |
| | Savings on health | Σ Health expenditure |
| | Job support | Σ (hours devoted * cost); expenditure |
| | R&D&I | Σ expenditure |
| | Transport | Σ subsidized expenditure |
| Third sector | Purchases from third sector entities | % average value added suppliers * total purchase volume |
| | Positive externalities | Σ expenditure on open projects |

**Table 6.7** Specific social value matrix for VVMM of Bilbao

| Stakeholder | Value variable | PROXYS | Relations algorithms |
|---|---|---|---|
| Users | Saving rents weighted | (Market rent − actual rent) * ratio * No income family members | Σ Savings rents weighted + spill |
| | Spill | Σ spending spill | |
| Neighbors | Social revitalization | Saving rent * friend | Social revitalization value * Urgan expenses |
| | Urban revitalization | Σ (Spill; Programs; Urban expenses) | |
| Citizenship | Solidarity | Saving in rents * Risk exclusion | Average saving with rents * occupied houses * Exclusion risk |
| | Economic return | Saving in the average savings * No occupied houses | |
| Industry entities | Externalities | Σ Externalities costs | Σ Externalities costs |

For the sake of illustration we take the cases of Lantegi Batuak and Viviendas Municipales de Bilbao. Tables 6.6 and 6.7 show the main characteristics of each analysis, along with the similarities and differences between them.

As can be seen, the two matrices run parallel in their categories, which are deduced from the Polyhedral Model. However, the stakeholders and the value variables identified are different, and therefore so are the proxies and the integration algorithms. Thus, all the processes of quantification share the same structure of analysis but they diverge in terms of the items valued. The more similar two organizations are in terms of their missions and the stakeholders for whom they generate value, the more similar their specific value matrices will be. And the more different they are, the more different their specific social value (SSV) matrices will be.

Blended social value is determined for each organization by consolidating the values generated for each stakeholder group in each of the three areas analyzed, i.e. social impact of economic activity (EASI), socio-economic return (S-ER), and specific social value (SSV).

## References

AECA Asociación Española de Contabilidad y Administración De Empresas (2002) Indicadores para la gestión Empresarial (Working paper no 17) Madrid, Spain. AECA Press. Retrieved 15 April 2013 from http://www.aeca.es/comisiones/comisionpg.htm

Argandoña A (1998) The stakeholder theory and the common good. J Bus Ethics 17(9–10): 1093–1102

Argandoña A (2011) Stakeholder theory and value creation. (Working paper IESE No. 9). Barcelona, Spain. IESE Business School

Davis JH, Schoorman FD, Donaldson L (1997) Toward a stewardship theory of management. Acad Manag Rev 22(1):20–47

Donaldson T, Dunfee TW (1994) Toward a unified conception of business ethics: integrative social contracts theory. Acad Manag Rev 19(2):252–284

Eisenhardt KM (1989) Building theories from case study research. Acad Manag Rev 14(4): 532–550

Emerson J, Wachowitz J, Chun S (2000) Social return on investment: exploring aspects of value creation in the nonprofit sector. Chapter 8, 131–173. The Robert Enterprise Development Fund. Retrieved 1 Nov 2013 from http://www.redf.com

Felber C (2012) La economía del bien común. Deusto, Barcelona

Freeman RE (1984) Strategic management: a stakeholder approach. Pitman, Boston

Freeman RE, Harrison JS, Wicks A (2008) Managing for stakeholders: survival, reputation, and success. Yale University Press, New Haven

Freeman RE, Harrison JS, Wicks AC, Parmar BL, De Colle S (2010) Stakeholder theory: the state of the art. Cambridge University Press, Cambridge

Gallizo JLG (2007) Valor económico y su distribución en los informes de sostenibilidad. AECA: Revista de la Asociación Española de Contabilidad y Administración de Empresas 78:34–37

Global Reporting Initiative (GRI) 4 (2013) G4 Sustainability reporting guidelines. Paper retrieved 10 Feb 2015 from https://www.globalreporting.org/resourcelibrary/GRIG4-Part1-Reporting-Principles-and-Standard-Disclosures.pdf

Goodpaster KE (1991) Business ethics and stakeholder analysis. Bus Ethics Q 1(01):53–73

Harris M, Raviv A (1978) Some results on incentive contracts with applications to education and employment, health insurance, and law enforcement. Am Econ Rev 20–30

Jensen MC (2001) Value maximization, stakeholder theory, and the corporate objective function. Eur Financ Manage 7:297–317

Jensen MC, Meckling WH (1976) Theory of the firm: managerial behavior, agency costs and ownership structure. J Financ Econ 3(4):305–360

Kaplan RS, Norton DP (2006) Alignment: using the balanced scorecard to create corporate synergies. Harvard Business Press, Boston

Kaufmann A, Gil Aluja J (1986) Introducción de la teoría de los subconjuntos borrosos a la gestión de las empresas. Santiago de Compostela, Spain, Milladoiro

Kennedy HMR (2013) Social media provides a megaphone for organizations intent on shaping the corporate environment. Strategy Leadersh 41(5):39–47

Melé D (2002) Not only stakeholder interests: the firm oriented toward the common good. In: Cortright SA, Naughton MJ (eds) Rethinking the purpose of business. Interdisciplinary essays from the Catholic Social Tradition. University of Notre Dame Press, Notre Dame, 190–214

Melé D (2009) The view and purpose of the firm in Freeman's stakeholder theory. Philos Manage 8:3–13

Moneva JM, Archel P, Correa C (2006) GRI and the camouflaging of corporate unsustainability. In: Accounting forum, vol 30(2). Elsevier, Amsterdam, pp 121–137

Peteraf MA (1993) The cornerstones of competitive advantage: a resource-based view. Strateg Manag J 14(3):179–191

Retolaza JL, San-Jose L (2011) Social economy and stakeholder theory, an integrative framework for socialization of the capitalism. CIRIEC-España, Revista de Economía Pública, Social y Cooperativa 73:193–213

Retolaza JL, Ruiz-Roqueñi M, San-Jose L (2015) An innovation approach to stakeholder theory: application in spanish transnational corporations. Revista Brasileira de Gestao de Negocios

Ruiz-Roqueñi M, Retolaza JL (2012) Stakeholder marketing: a new orientation in the discipline and practice of marketing. J Mod Acc Auditing 8(6):811–826

San-Jose L, Retolaza JL (2012) Participation of stakeholders in corporate governance: foundation ontological and methodological proposal. Universitas Psychol 11(2):619–628

Sison AJG, Fontrodona J (2012) The common good of the firm in the Aristotelian-Thomistic tradition. Bus Ethics Q 22(02):211–246

Smith A (1776) The wealth of nations. In: Edwin C (ed) (1904) Reprint. Modern Library, New York, 1937. And Smith A (1991) The wealth of nations, vol 3. Skinner AS (ed) Prometheus Books, New York, NY

Zadeh LA (1965) Fuzzy sets. Inf Control 8:338–353

# Chapter 7
# Process Model Analysis and Calculation: Spoly

**Abstract** This chapter develops the process of calculating the monetary value of social value based on the "Polyhedral Model", which consists of six steps. In step one the process begins with the identification of the working team and the setting of the timetable. Step two involves work on the strategic and management documents of the organization, ending with the preparation of a consensus-based stakeholder map. Step three focuses on identifying the value variables perceived by stakeholders, mainly through phenomenological interviews, and ends with the preparation of the Value Variables Matrix (VVM) for the organization. Step four identifies the outputs generated by the organization for each value variable and seeks potential proxies which, after a process of fuzzy calculation, enable reference values to be identified for the respective outputs. Step five entails the quantification of the calculations as per the "Polyhedral Model", making it possible to see the value generated for each stakeholder, the shared value and the consolidated value in numerical and graphic forms. The sixth and final step is a review of the whole process and the proposal of improvements for the next calculation cycle, which generally coincides with the next financial year.

**Keywords** Social accounting · Polyhedral model · Consolidated value · Blended value · Stakeholder map · Phenomenological interview · Proxys · SPOLY

There are three clearly distinct though interlinked parts involved in monetizing social value at organizations: first there is the underlying Polyhedral Model as explained in-depth above; then there is the process of analysis, which we look at in this chapter. Lastly there is the creation of a consensus-based system of potential proxies that can be selected systematically to quantify outputs. This last part is referred to here through specific examples, but the registration and systemizing of a set of proxies goes beyond university level and requires the joint effort of a real community of users. Hopefully such a community can be created and organized sooner rather than later.

Figure 7.1 sums up the successive steps and the outputs that result from them. These provide the inputs for the next stage of the process. The technical resources generally used in each stage of the process are also noted.



J.L. Retolaza et al., *Social Accounting for Sustainability*,
SpringerBriefs in Business, DOI 10.1007/978-3-319-13377-5_7

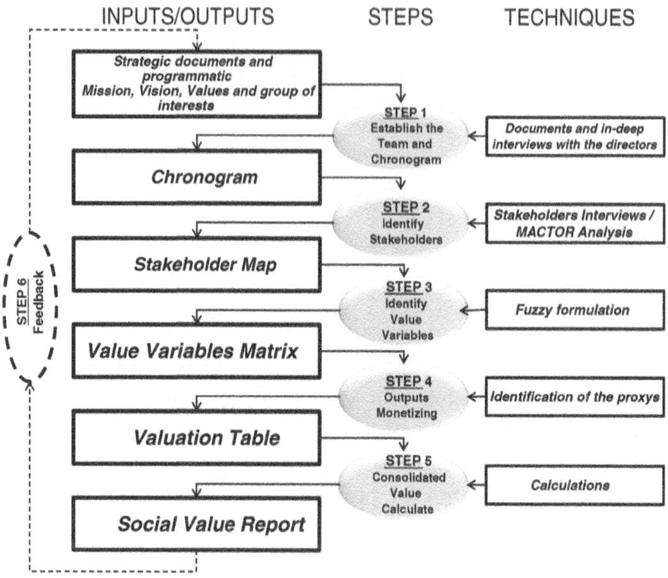


**Fig. 7.1** Process model of analysis

## 7.1 Establishing Teams and Calendars

The process usually begins when someone in authority at an organization decides that it would be useful to quantify the social value that it generates. In our experience the reasons behind this decision are generally linked to reputation or communication issues. Once such a system has been developed it becomes an important management tool, but it is not usually seen as such at the outset.

Next, the organization must decide whether to undertake the process itself or to bring in external support, usually in the form of a consultancy firm or a university. The materials developed are open source (available at www.geaccounting.org), and if the organization in question is similar in structure to any of the templates already drawn up it can manage the process itself or with the aid of a consultancy firm familiar with the model. If it is necessary to develop a new model of analysis the organization may enlist the help of a university. In any event universities can always be called into generate processes of accompaniment and transfer of know-how.

The team assigned to the task should include at least two members of the organization, or three if no external support is to be brought in. If possible they should be management staff from the financial and social areas. As in any other process of change, the project must be taken on board by the organization as a whole and led by the top management.

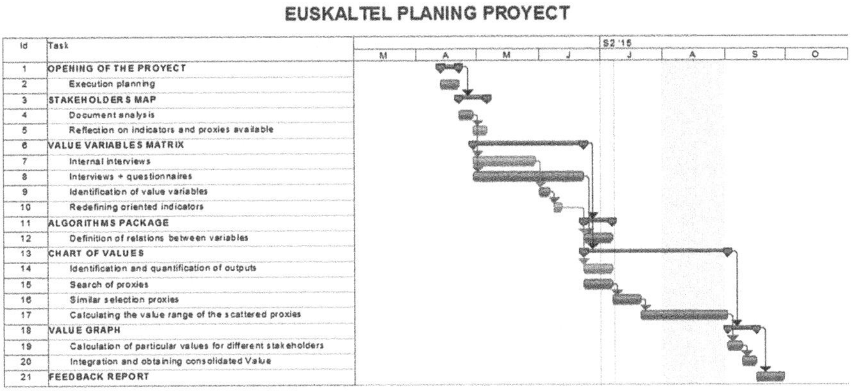


**Fig. 7.2** Calendar for a project: the case of Euskaltel

This initial stage can be thought of as an orientation period. It can be considered to have ended once the team is formally set up and the calendar for work is approved. Figure 7.2 shows a fairly typical calendar established by telephone operator Euskaltel. The average duration of projects is six months, though it may be as little as three or as much as a year depending on the circumstances. Although this is perhaps the simplest stage in methodological terms, it also tends to be the longest because of the in-depth interviews held with stakeholder representatives.

## 7.2 Identifying Stakeholder Groups

Once the team has been formed and the calendar approved, the next stage is to draw up the stakeholder map of the organization. This is based on both the implicit knowledge held by those involved in the project and the explicit knowledge provided by strategic and program documents such as the company vision, its strategy plan and its quality reports. The drawing up of this map is not a one-off action but rather a process: the team prepares a draft document that is then checked out with the various interlocutors so that each one can contribute to it. The map is not completed until a consensus is reached as to its correctness. It is advisable to use a mind-mapping program (Mindjet, Freemind, Novamind, etc.) to help prepare and consolidate the map.

The Fig. 7.3 shows the stakeholder map of the Basque Mining Museum, drawn up using Mindjet. The figure below shows the map of the Argia foundation, drawn up as a PowerPoint presentation. Two points must be made concerning stakeholder maps: on the one hand they are based on the viewpoint of value generated in the

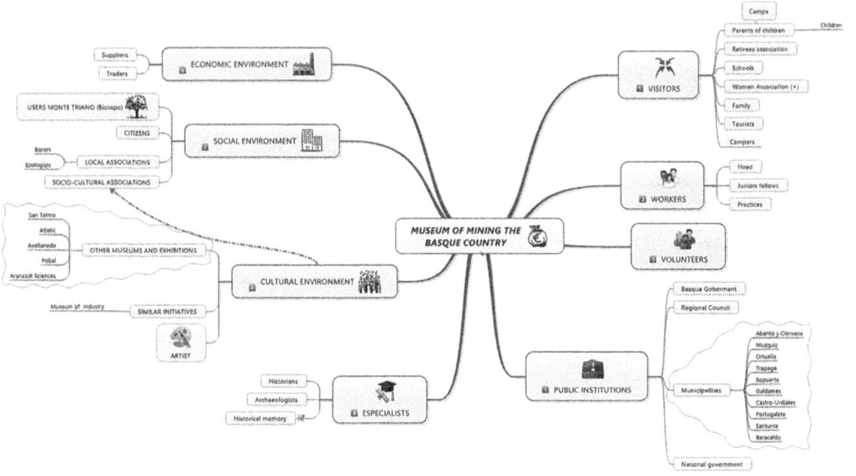


**Fig. 7.3** Stakeholder map: the case of the Basque Mining Museum

past rather than future strategy, so they do not necessarily coincide with the designs that would have emerged in the strategic planning framework. The clearest example of such differences can be found in non-strategic suppliers, who are hard to include in strategy maps but should be included in social valuation maps because the purchases that the organization makes from them generate value not just for the supplier but also for society as a whole via the socio-economic return on part of the value added for the administration in the form of taxes, etc. On the other hand there is no need to worry too much about being exhaustive, because these are additive procedures so any stakeholders who have been omitted can be added later (though this should be the exception rather than the rule).

The next step is to identify potential interlocutors in each group of stakeholders identified. The Fig. 7.4 shows the specific identification of the different organizations that make up stakeholder groups; now it is necessary to identify a specific individual at each organization with which discussions are to be held. As a general rule, the interlocutors selected should be at the core of each reference group and should be knowledgeable concerning the value that may potentially be generated by the organization conducting the analysis. The number of interviewees is limited only by the time available, but at least one interlocutor per stakeholder group should be interviewed. Our experience leads us to deduce that between 15 and 20 is an appropriate number of interviews for a medium-sized organization, but the key lies in covering all the value variables that may arise in regard to the different stakeholders. The more homogenous the stakeholders are, the fewer interviews are required, and the more heterogeneous they are (and therefore the more likely it is that different members of any given group may perceive different value variables) the more interviews need to be held. Questionnaires could be used to reach larger numbers of interlocutors.

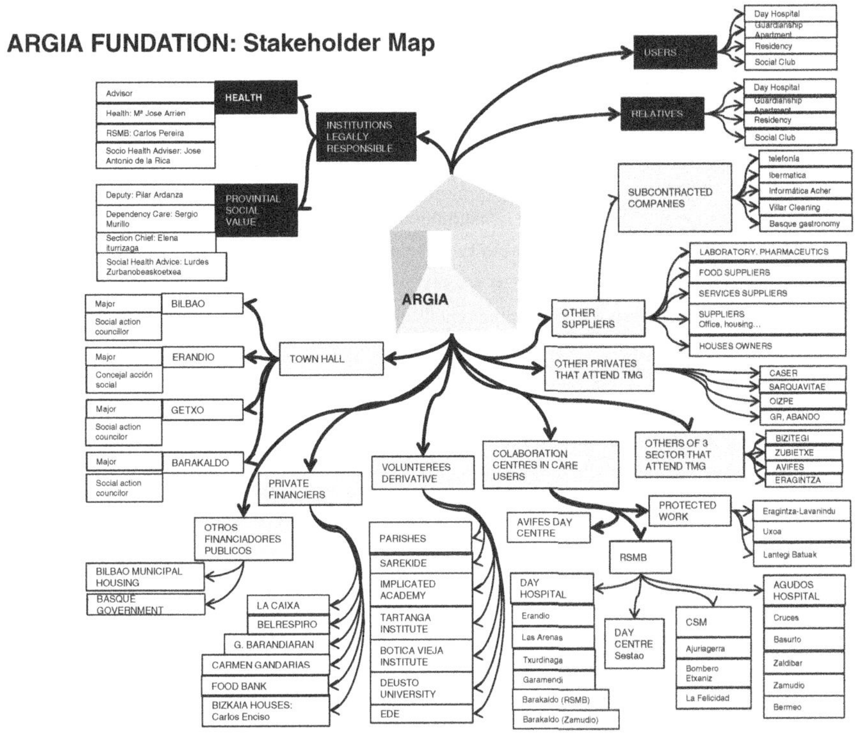


**Fig. 7.4** Stakeholder map: Argia foundation

## 7.3 Identifying Value Variables

Apart from the identification of proxies, interviews are perhaps the issue that gives rise to most doubts prior to the commencement of the process, even though conducting them may well then turn out to be one of its simplest parts. The complexity lies in arranging them.

The first doubt that arises is who should conduct the interview: someone from the organization, someone from the consultancy firm or perhaps someone from the University. The answer depends on three factors: the first is the balance between financial resources and personnel with time available at the organization. If the former outweighs the latter, it is advisable to resort to external interviewers, but if the latter outweighs the former they should be conducted internally. The second factor is concerned with the image that the organization wishes to convey to its interlocutors (with whom it usually has important links); the use of external interviewers, especially if they are drawn from a university, gives the impression of commitment to the project and rigorous analysis, while in-house interviewers give an impression of proximity and greater internal involvement. The third factor is "bracketing" or "phenomenological époché", i.e. the idea that the interviewer must approach the

**Table 7.1** Value variables: Formació y Treball

| Value variables identified by stakeholders | |
|---|---|
| 1 | Create work and helps employability in key social cohesion |
| 2 | Learning and training offices |
| 3 | Self-esteem and confidence |
| 4 | Career counseling |
| 5 | Increased income and personal consumption |
| 6 | Ability to feel useful and opportunity to be active |
| 7 | Reward for providing a service to society |
| 8 | Promotion and promoting recycling; catalysts for change model; process innovation and improvement in the management of textile recycling |
| 9 | Transparency and adaptability |
| 10 | Reducing $CO_2$ emissions |
| 11 | Jurisdiction and efficiency in fulfilling its mission |
| 12 | Instrument to support the common goals |
| 13 | Own initiative and innovation |
| 14 | Savings generated by the clothing collection service |
| 15 | Favor compliance with legislation |
| 16 | Dignity and social service dining |
| 17 | Channeling social services checks |
| 18 | Return to social work |
| 19 | Generated economic performance and brand image |
| 20 | Accredited and professional training certificates; transfer of know-how in integration processes; offer competitive training market |
| 21 | Regarding tractor and social sector entity insertion companies |
| 22 | Value added training for specific communities |
| 23 | Ability to lobby and business generation capacity shared |
| 24 | Advice and knowledge in managing the end of life cycle of the textile and reuse |
| 25 | Supporting CSR policies; communicative and informative value |
| 26 | Product quality and professionalism as a supplier; advice for start-up 2nd hand stores |

interviewee without prejudice and with a willingness to listen from zero (blank slate). This is normally easier to achieve with external interviewers, who have less knowledge of and emotional commitment to the organization. Annex I below gives a script for interviews, and Annex II gives a template for an online questionnaire.

When the interviews with interlocutors at stakeholders and, if relevant, the questionnaires have been completed a set of value variables has been identified. After a process of integration of synonymous expressions, this gives rise to a list such as the one in Table 7.1, taken from the firm Formació i Treball.

Next comes what is perhaps the most complex stage of the process: redefining the variables expressed in general terms in the form of indicators corresponding to measurable outputs of the organization, with the implication that proxies can be obtained to value those outputs in monetary terms (Table 7.2).

**Table 7.2** Allocation of social value variables to stakeholders

US: users
W: workers
V: volunteers
G: Government
SO: social organizations
BP: business partners
C: clients
U: universities
E: environment

| | STAKEHOLDERS | | | | | | | | |
|---|---|---|---|---|---|---|---|---|---|
| VALUE VARIABLE | US. | W. | V. | G. | S.O. | B.P. | C. | U. | E. |
| Employee access to persons in exclusion risk | ■ | | | ■ | | | | | |
| Training Development | ■ | | | ■ | ■ | | | | |
| Employee skills development | ■ | | | ■ | ■ | | | | |
| Improving purchaising power | ■ | | | | | | | | |
| Saving with public benefits | | | | ■ | | | | | |
| Generating Stable Employment | | ■ | | | | | | | |
| Social Delivery | ■ | | | ■ | | | | | |
| Voluntary Participation | | | ■ | | | | | | |
| Textile Waste utilization | | | | ■ | | ■ | | | ■ |
| Raise awareness of textile waste utilization | | | | ■ | | ■ | | | ■ |
| Savings in waste management costs (textile companies | | | | | | ■ | | | ■ |
| Use of other waste | | | | ■ | | ■ | | | ■ |
| Savings in waste management costs (savings management) | | | | ■ | | | | | ■ |
| Reducing CO2 emissions by recycling textile waste | | | | ■ | | ■ | | | ■ |
| Generating innovative solutions (tractor effect) | | | | ■ | | ■ | ■ | ■ | |
| Trust | | | | ■ | | | ■ | ■ | |
| Creation of shared business | | | | | ■ | | | | |
| Know-How Transference | | | | | ■ | | ■ | ■ | ■ |

## 7.4 Identifying and Monetizing Outcomes

Once these variables—which will be different for each company or at least each type of company—are obtained it is necessary to identify the outputs generated by the organization that correspond to each variable, and the proxies that enable them to be quantified. The Tables 7.3 and 7.4 show the outputs for the Lantegi Batuak foundation.

The categories shown in this first table refer entirely to the social impacts generated through economic or trading operations, i.e. what we have called socio-economic value. This is divided into three types: (1) direct, i.e. generated via value added or its equivalent; (2) indirect, i.e. generated via purchases from suppliers, in which not all the expenditure is considered but only the value added in line with its distribution in society by those suppliers (wages, personal income tax, social security payments, and other taxation); and (3) the value generated for clients themselves via transfers of value, applicable only to special employment organizations and those whose invoicing per hour is below the average cost per hour for the sector. In this specific case, this refers to the social economy, which is identified

**Table 7.3** Social value indicators: Lantegi Batuak

| Socio-economic value of commercial activity | | | |
|---|---|---|---|
| Socio-economic value live | Socio-economic value indirectly: suppliers | Socio-economic value indirect: customers | Socio-economic value indirectly: social economy |
| Indicator | Indicator | Indicator | Indicator |
| Value added | Purchase suppliers (by geographical area of reference) | Average wage cost entity | Purchase suppliers in the territory of reference |
| Wages | Total turnover of suppliers | Average wage cost reference level (national, local) | Total turnover of social economy suppliers |
| Social security | Staff costs | Check local customers | Staff costs |
| Income tax | Value added | Staff costs | Value added |
| Value added tax | Operating results | Value added | Operating results |
| Another tax | Corporation tax | Operating results | Tax |
| Economic result | Undistributed profits | Corporation tax | |
| Surplus reinvested | | Undistributed profits | |

**Table 7.4** Indicators for social value with economic impact

| Specific indicators of social value | | | | |
|---|---|---|---|---|
| Saving for public administration | Value for families | Value for families | Positive externalities | Grant |
| Indicator | Indicator | Indicator | Indicator | |
| Non-contributory pension > 65 % disability | Psychics > 65 % | Number of occupational service users | Proyect 1 | A. General |
| Right to family care | Psychics > 33 % | Percentage who would be with family | Proyect 2 | B. Social object |
| Health benefits | Physical > 65 % | Food cost (ref. Lantegi) | Proyect 3 | C. Specific social objectives |
| Transition to standard employment | Physical > 33 % | Day dining year of use | | D. Private donations and aids |
| Employment Creation (Special Employment Centre) | No. of working days | Health workforce | | |
| Standard Job Creation | Average working hours per worker | Occupational service | | |
| | Average wage cost worker with mental disability | Special Employment Center | | |
| | Average wage cost physically disabled worker | Personal without disabilities | | |
| | Average worker wage cost without disabilities | | | |

as a specific stakeholder of this foundation and is interested in learning how much in economic terms the organization contributes to it.

The second table shows indicators related to the return for the public administration attained via savings, which must be added to the returns generated via the socio-economic value variables (social security payments, personal income tax and other taxation). The remaining variables refer to the specific social value, in this case generated for users, families and similar organizations. Finally, the amount received in subsidies is shown at the bottom of the last column. This amount is used to find the net value generated once subsidies are subtracted from the gross value.

Information on the outputs generated for each variable must be sought by the organization itself. Sometimes there may be data that can be obtained but in this case no such data was included explicitly in the design of the management system, so there is not. In cases such as this all that can be done is to indicate the output and include it in the system of indicators of the organization so that data can be recorded in future years for inclusion in the monetization process. It must be pointed out here that although the monetization process may take an average of six months in the first year, as indicated above, in future years a single day should suffice. This may not be true of all future years, because as time passes the value variables and the proxies used to quantify them may presumably vary, making it necessary to repeat at least part of the phenomenological comparison process. This in-depth analysis should be carried out when significant changes are perceived to have taken place in the working environment or in the organization itself. A useful pointer is to conduct the analysis when changes are made in the design of the organization's strategy, though it could also be conducted the following year so as to stagger the effort involved.

The next problem is selecting the proxies: Once an output has been identified that can be fitted into a value variable, one or more monetary proxies must be found that enable it to be quantified in monetary terms. Costs and savings on the part of the public administration usually make good proxies because they identify what the administration, as a representative of society, is willing to pay for the relevant outputs.

However, there is usually not a single proxy but rather a set of them. The creation of new jobs can be taken as an example: An analysis of what the public administration has paid in recent years to create jobs reveals figures of between zero and €6000. When it comes to choosing the most suitable proxy, various strategies can be adopted. The simplest is to choose the proxy that is most similar to the output generated. For example, for Lantegi Batuak it seems logical to choose a proxy from the Basque Country or, better still, from Bizkaia (the province in which the foundation is based and conducts most of its operations) in regard to job creation for disabled persons or persons with particular difficulties in finding employment. The proxy chosen needs to be up-to-date or at least as recent as possible. Thus, proxies need to be similar to outputs in both timing and place. In this case, spending by the Basque Government on the creation of jobs for persons with particular difficulties in finding employment is made via job placement companies, and may therefore seem like a good proxy, even though, following a criterion of prudence, the value of the output exceeds that of the proxy because the latter refers to jobs that last three years while jobs created at Lantegi Batuak are for an indefinite period. Moreover, in successive years the value attributed to new jobs created must be reduced by the value of jobs destroyed, applying the same accounting considerations but in the opposite direction.

In other cases the proxy is an idealized measure based on the analysis of a set of specific proxies. To help readers understand this mechanism a typical proxy from the Formació i Treball (FiT) project is calculated below: the quantification of the social value of 1 tonne of reused solid waste.

Figure 7.5 is based on the data in the table shown. A widespread in value can be seen, so to obtain a typical value the lateral outriders that distort the normality of the graph are discarded. A centroid score is then selected in the form of the median, which is more stable than the average. This score gives a value of €62, and this is the figure that we take as our reference.

Once a numerical value is determined for the outputs that can be considered as outcomes by virtue of the phenomenological method (stakeholder perception), and once a proxy has been selected—understood as an item of comparison with the benchmark monetary value—(be it a single specific proxy or a typical proxy obtained via a function of belonging) the next step is to identify the relational algorithm that links the two items. This often takes the form of a multiplication, with the value generated for each variable then being calculated. The Table 7.5 is an example taken from Formació i Treball.

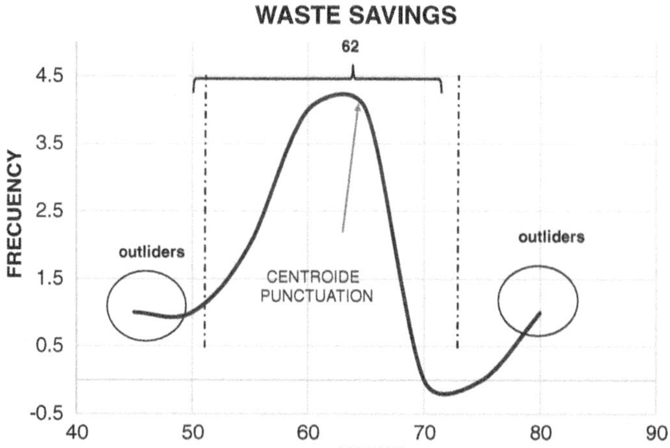


| Beula (Olot) | Osona | Clariana Cardener | Bages | Roses | Baix Empordá | Alt Empordá | Abrera | La Segarra | Lloret | Área de Tarragona | Barcelona |
|---|---|---|---|---|---|---|---|---|---|---|---|
| 46,9 | 52,3 | 55,8 | 58,4 | 60,9 | 61,5 | 62 | 64,4 | 65,2 | 67,1 | 68,4 | 83 |

**Fig. 7.5** Fuzzy logic: quantification of waste

**Table 7.5** Relational algorithms: the case of Formació i Treball

| Value variables | Indicator | Indicator value | Algorithm | Proxy | Resource | Proxy value | Monetary value |
|---|---|---|---|---|---|---|---|
| Voluntary | Voluntary number of hours | 17.22 | Number of hours of volunteer * time volunteering price | Hour Price for being a volunteer market value, less income tax and workers tax | FiT accountability | 8.17 € | 140.687 |
| Social delivery | Assigned economic value | 448.263 | I Economic Value assigned to Social Delivery Programme | | FiT accountability | | 448.263 |
| Generation of innovative solutions | Innovative project number | 8 | (Iinvestments + Icurrent expenses) innovative projects | | FiT | | 3.450.918 € |
| Trust and transparency | Containernumbers instaled without economic payment compensation | 500 | No. of containers * canon | Municipal canon for the container placement | Gava Council Sheets, 2014 | 400 | 200 |
| | No. m2 leased local/ships under a grant of use | 3.4 | M2 No * comercial building market value | Average monthly price to the m2 in building rental | Industrial market report Catalunya, 2-S 2013 Forcadell estates | 3.42 € | 139.536 |
| | No. m2 of land leased out under assignment of use | 2.75 | M2 No * solar market value * 5 % (long-term property value) | Average selling price of the m2 of industrial sites in Barcelones | Industrial market report Catalunya, 2-S 2013 Forcadell estates | 234,20 € | 32.203 |

(continued)

**Table 7.5** (continued)

| Value variables | Indicator | Indicator value | Algorithm | Proxy | Resource | Proxy value | Monetary value |
|---|---|---|---|---|---|---|---|
| Generating shared business | Economic volume of shared plans | 1.467.592 € | Sum of the value generated by joint projects (Roba Amiga and Nouset) | Suitable for economic value for FIT shared projects | FiT accountability | | 1.467.592 € |
| Transfer of know-how | No hours spent on projects for external collaboration | | | | | | |

## 7.5 Calculation and Viewing of Value

The Fig. 7.6 shows the social value generated by Viviendas Municipales de Bilbao, broken down into the three ecosystems mentioned above. On the one hand there is an economic benefit that says little about the social value generated and is merely a supplementary measure, and on the other hand the three ecosystems of social value can be seen: (1) the value generated for society as a whole by the economic operations of the organization; (2) the money returned to the public administration through payments and savings; and (3) the specific social value generated for the various stakeholders, who in this case are mainly tenants and the general public. The consolidated value—which is similar to the accounting item of the same name—takes into account the joint value generated, avoiding any duplication of the shared value generated at the same time for more than one stakeholder for more than one ecosystem.

The percentages shown referred to the ratio of the total value generated in the corresponding ecosystem to the value of the fixed assets in the form of housing held by the organization. It is therefore a social profitability ratio covering the full set of homes managed. This may be important in interpreting the returns of the organization.

The Fig. 7.7 shows the social results of Lantegi Batuak; it must be mentioned that the ecosystems do not always follow the same order in terms of size. Indeed, at Lantegi Batuak the order is the reverse of that at Vivendas Municipales de Bilbao. In this figure the percentage shown in each circle represents the result of dividing the value generated by the public subsidies received in regard to each ecosystem. It therefore shows the return on each Euro provided by the public administration. As can be seen, the ratios in each report are not standardized but are rather decided according to the peculiarities of each organization and its needs for feedback and communication. Finally, the amount shown on the right in brackets is the net value generated once the public subsidies received have been subtracted from the gross value.

Finally, it must be pointed out that the value generated is not homogenous, as it is distributed across the set of stakeholders. Figure 7.8 referring to Formació i Treball,

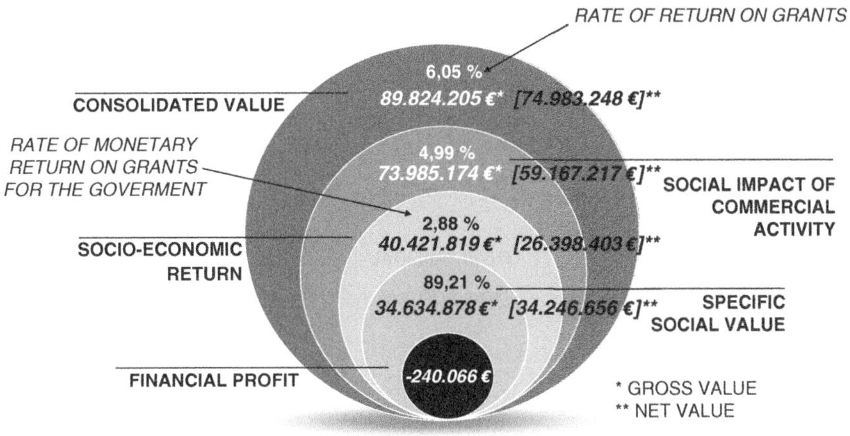


**Fig. 7.6** Social value generated: The case of Viviendas Municipales de Bilbao

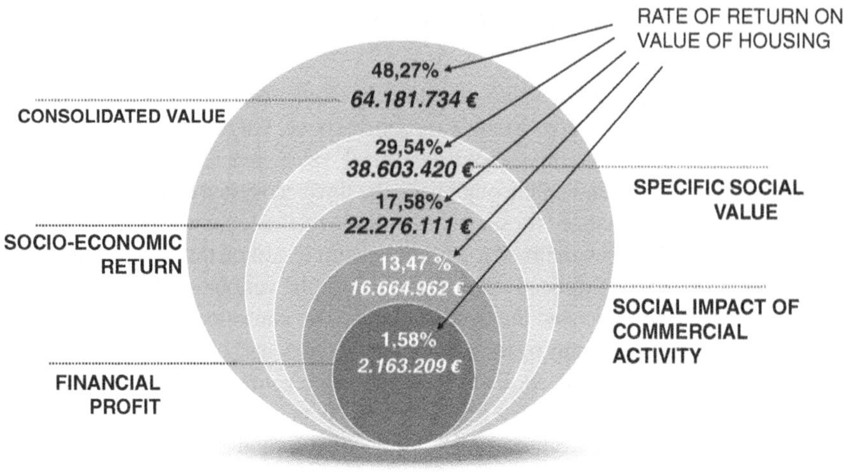


**Fig. 7.7** Social value generated: the case of Lantegi Batuak

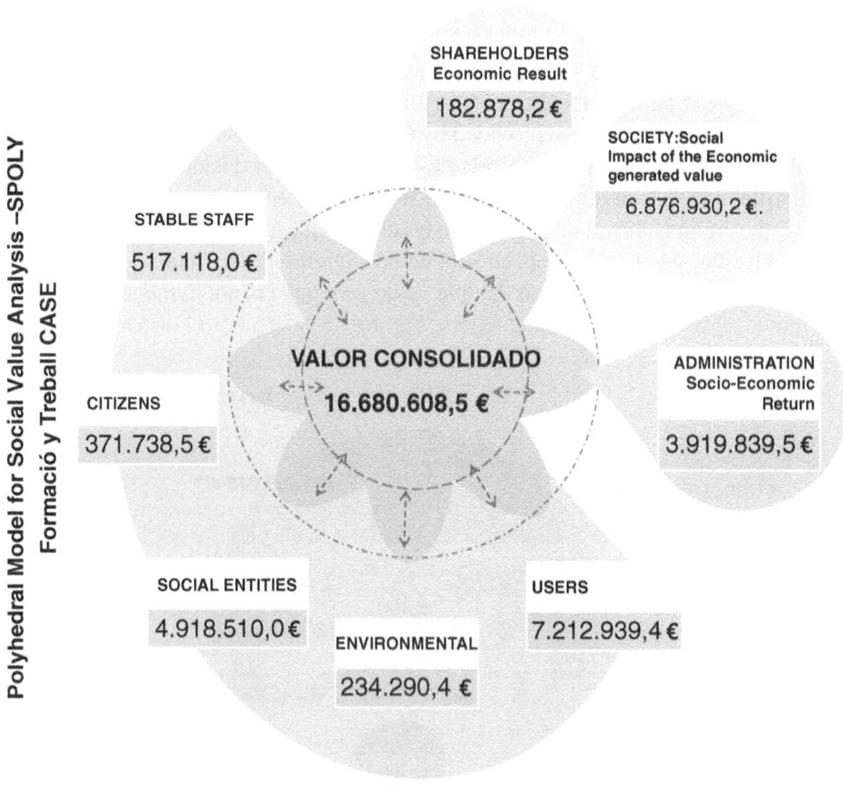


**Fig. 7.8** SPOLY at Formación i Treball

shows the social value generated not only per ecosystem but also per stakeholder. This provides a better view of the value generated, as the proportion of value distributed can be seen separately, allowing analysis to focus on the part that corresponds to the mission of the organization, or on the balance of distribution itself. Although FiT is structured as a company, it is user-oriented in terms of its mission. It can be seen that the value generated for users is €7,212,939.40, which is equivalent to a little more than 100 % of its turnover. The analyses that can be run include the calculation of the ratio of internal to external value generated and the rate of return for the administration, which in this case would be 223 %. Considering that these rates are never absolute, they do not provide much information unless they can be compared. Two types of analysis can be conducted: a comparison of the year-on-year trends of benchmark rates, and an analysis of the balance in the distribution of value to different stakeholders. With a view to the future, once a community of users has been set up progress can be made towards benchmarking processes on a sectoral basis or per type of organization.

As stated above, firms that conduct social accounting currently tend to do so from a reputational viewpoint. However the monetization of social value also serves to identify a number of indicators that can subsequently be incorporated into the management system on the same level as financial indicators, enabling social value to become a core part of management. In this way social issues can become part of the backbone of an organization.

# Chapter 8
# Conclusions

**Abstract** There is increasing demand in society for the social impact generated by organizations to be measured. Monetizing it and integrating it with economic/financial information so as to optimize the sustainability of organizations themselves and of the socioeconomic system in which they operate is a major challenge. This paper identifies the problem and the main lines proposed for solving it to date. Based on the analytic-synthetic method and on cost-benefit analysis, and making four prior methodological assumptions—action research, stakeholder theory, a phenomenological outlook and fuzzy logic—a model is proposed for interpreting and monetizing the social value generated by organizations. The method proposed involves three distinct parts: first of all an underlying interpretative model called the Polyhedral Model, drawn up on the basis of considering organizations as networks of stakeholders who share resources and risks in order to generate some kind of joint economic, social or emotional value that is then distributed in a shared or individual fashion among those stakeholders. Secondly there is a practical model or application known as SPOLY, which comprises six steps structures to enable all types of trading, public-sector and social organizations to calculate the value that they generate for their stakeholders. Finally there is a proxy-based weighting system applied specifically to groups of variables. Altogether the method proposed can be seen as a new model of social accounting for sustainability.

**Keywords** Social accounting · Polyhedral model · SPOLY · Monetizing social value · Sustainability · Value for stakeholders

Perhaps as a result of the crisis, the public are currently increasing concerned about the social value created or destroyed by organizations in both the social economy and the mercantile economy. These effects are felt most in larger firms, particularly in transnational companies. Any move in this direction, as proposed by the European Union and various international organizations, requires that organizations be capable of objectifying and weighting their social value, and of blending that value with their economic results to provide a complete view of the blended value that they generate. The concept of comparative social value promoted by the EU, the GRI and the Integrated Reporting Framework follows the same line.



J.L. Retolaza et al., *Social Accounting for Sustainability*,
SpringerBriefs in Business, DOI 10.1007/978-3-319-13377-5_8

However, a paradigm is needed that is capable of providing support for conceptualization and measurement of social value. The two paradigms that currently prevail—the neo-liberal paradigm and the common good—pose problems that are hard to solve. The combination of a phenomenological approach with stakeholder theory enables a process of objectification and weighting of the social value created by organizations to be set up. This theoretical approach is then developed using the theory of fuzzy sets to generate the Polyhedral Model, which enables us to identify the inputs and outputs that must be taken into account for quantitative and qualitative evaluation of the value generated to be carried out.

Few studies of the objectification of social value currently exist, and even those are mostly concerned with intervention. A wide range of techniques is used, but with little in the way of a theoretical framework. The Polyhedral Model enables the set of inputs and outputs selected to be explained. On the basis of those inputs and outputs a cost-benefit analysis method can be used in which social inputs and outputs can be monetized. The mechanisms used are the same ones employed in accounting to obtain reasonable values: first, the market price, if any; second, shadow pricing; and third, plausible indicators of value. It must be taken into account that the range of reasonable social values is much broader than in the case of financial values, which increases the fuzziness of the system and requires that a community of users be created which can, by consensus, gradually delimit the breadth of that range.

The result obtained has been checked out at a small number of organizations covering both social and mercantile areas. It provides a qualification of the social value generated for each stakeholder, and thus of the consolidated value for the full set of stakeholders. The value obtained enables the same type of unit (in this case the euro) to be used to quantify both economic value and a large part of social value. This certainly provides a better view of the overall value generated by a given organization, and makes it easier to integrate both economic and social goals into its management system. It also enables a comparative analysis to be run not just of social value per se but also of the blended value generated by different organizations. This means that the efficiency levels of different organizations can be compared regardless of whether they are mercantile, social, public-sector or non-profit. An example of the possibilities that this opens up is a comparative analysis of efficiency in the creation of value between banks and savings banks in Spain over the past 10 years (San-Jose et al. 2014); another is a comparison of start-ups and consolidated firms (Retolaza et al. 2015).

Finally, if the weighting of the social value generated can be systematized and generalized then it can be integrated into the GDP or into a similar, more inclusive indicator to provide a much more comprehensive view of the actual value generated by a given country.

The main limitation of this study is that if it is to be effective then, as occurs with the accounting system, internationally recognized standards must be drawn up for a objectifying and weighting social value. Accordingly, this study is just another brick put towards building such a regulatory system. For more than five centuries people have been working to improve the accounting systems used to reflect and set down the economic value of organizations, and even so progress is still being made in accounting standards. It is to be hoped that quicker progress can be made in drawing up standards for social valuation, but a broad range of researchers and managers will need to work as a network on the matter, and a considerable time will be required to draw up a combination for comparing hypotheses with the trial and error method. This will certainly also call for the involvement of practitioners not just to implement the social accounting system at their companies and organizations but to draw up a community of users capable of moving towards standardization, particularly in terms of the proxies to be used.

This necessary contribution to the development of social accounting is certainly the main line of research that is being opened up here. The number of cases assessed needs to be increased, and the models and techniques best suited to this assessment need to be standardized.

## References

San-Jose L, Retolaza JL, Pruñonosa JT (2014) Efficiency in Spanish banking: a multistakeholder approach analysis. J Int Finan Markets Institutions Money 32:240–255

Retolaza, J.L.; San-Jose, L: & Torres-Pruñonosa, J. (2015). Socio-economic return of start-up companies: an advantage of Entrepreneurship. In: Peris-Ortiz M, Sahut J-M (eds) New challenges in entrepreneurship and finance. Examining the prospects for sustainable business development, performance, innovation, and economic growth. Heidelberg, Springer, pp. 259–271

# Annex I

## Analysis of Value Generated for Stakeholders Introduction for Interview

Thanks for agreeing to meet.
Explanation of the project:

1. Interest of the organization
   The organization to which I belong is attempting to analyze the social value that it generates for its stakeholders as a whole, and the extent to which it is possible to monetize the relevant impact. We sincerely believe that this can give us a better understanding of our role in our setting, and help us to make progress in the management and optimization of the social value that we generate.
2. Role of the interviewee
   You have been selected because you belong to one of the key stakeholder groups for our organization. We would like you to answer some questions on behalf of your own organization, but do not wish you to answer as a representative of anyone else.
3. Background
   This analysis is linked to the strategy plan that we have implemented this year. Our intention is not for it to be just a report, but to integrate it into our organization every year as social accounting.
4. Method
   The method used is the "Polyhedral Model", developed jointly by Deusto University and the University of the Basque Country. This method has been tried out at other local organizations such as Lantegi Batuak and Katea Legaia. We are the first organization in … to use it.
5. Goals of the interview
   The purpose of this interview is to learn your opinion concerning the value that our organization provides to you. We are not seeking complex, elaborate replies but merely a simple, spontaneous answer as to whether our organization contributes any value to you, and if so what that value is.



J.L. Retolaza et al., *Social Accounting for Sustainability*,
SpringerBriefs in Business, DOI 10.1007/978-3-319-13377-5

# Analysis of Value Generated for Stakeholders Script for Interview

Thanks for agreeing to meet.
Explanation of the project:

6. Interest of the organization
7. Role of the interviewee
8. Background
9. Method
10. Goals of the interview

We do not want you to give a general assessment of the organization but merely to refer to the value that you perceive.

(I) ***Could you please indicate the main points in which you believe that … generates value*** (for you as a person in the case of individual stakeholders or for your organization if you represent one)

Can you give me an example?
[If the interviewee is stuck, it may be useful to ask about specific anecdotes in which the value generated by the organization can be perceived]

(II) ***Could you identify any characteristics that could increase the value generated/perceived?***

Can you give me an example?

(III) ***Can you think of any indicators that could be used to identify the value generated?***

(IV) ***Can you think of any monetary quantification that could be used as a reference?***

(V) ***Would you like to add any comments or ideas of your own concerning the social value generated ought not generated by the organization in question?***

Thank the interviewee for his/her help and inform him/her that you will send a copy of the data when it becomes available.

Say goodbye

## DATA COLLECTION TABLE

| Perceived Value | Complementary Characteristics | proxys | Quantification |
|---|---|---|---|
| For example employment creation | For example full time<br>For example part time<br>For permanent contracts | For example No of permanent contracts | for example grant for insertion working |
| | | | |
| | | | |
| | | | |
| | | | |

This is a semi-structured interview, so room must be left for any ideas or contributions that the interviewee puts forward.

Most interviewees are only able to answer the first and second questions. The third and fourth should be regarded as supplementary, only for those interviewees who proved capable of responding in most depth on this matter.

It may often prove impossible to ask the questions directly: depending on the rank of the interviewee, questions may need to be posed more specifically. If the interviewee gets stuck it may be useful to ask him/her a "how" question to prompt him/her to tell a success or failure story involving the relationship between the organizations and describe what needs to happen for that relationship to be maintained.

The manufacturer's authorised representative in the EU is Springer Nature Customer Service Centre GmbH, Europaplatz 3, 69115 Heidelberg, Germany. If you have any concerns regarding our products, please contact ProductSafety@springernature.com

Printed and bound by CPI Group (UK) Ltd, Croydon, CR0 4YY
30/09/2026
02225606-0007